Within Reach

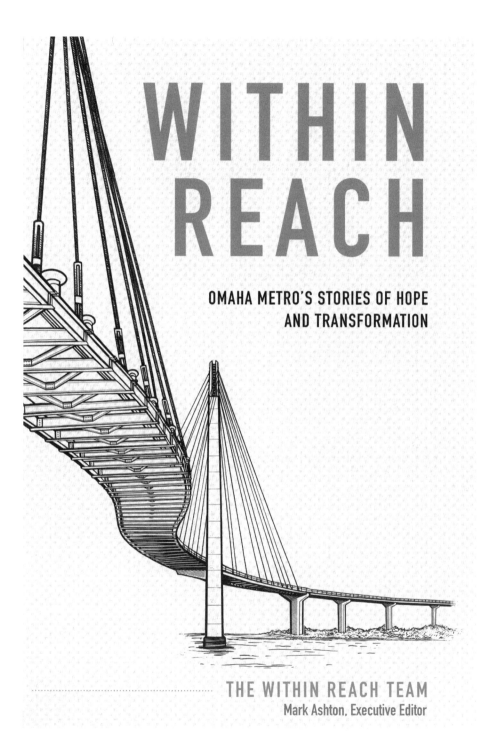

WITHIN REACH

OMAHA METRO'S STORIES OF HOPE AND TRANSFORMATION

THE WITHIN REACH TEAM
Mark Ashton, Executive Editor

Printed in United States of America
ISBN 978-0-9909222-8-5

Table of Contents

Introduction

The Within Reach Team

The Omaha Metro is an amazing place. Not only because it is home to the College World Series, Creighton University and the world's best zoo. Not simply because it is rated the best place in America to raise a family. Not just because it is the home to Union Pacific, Con Agra, TD Ameritrade, Kiewit and Berkshire Hathaway.

Omaha is a great place for spiritual and personal vitality. Thriving churches in Omaha do the unthinkable—they work together to see individuals and even large parts of the city experience personal transformation. Economic, educational, social and spiritual transformation are common in these corners of the city.

Within Reach is a network of over 30 churches that are poor and rich, white and black, educated and simple, young and old, wild, free, jubilant and stayed. They have broken down the walls of tradition and denominationalism to keep the main thing the main thing – and to impact our city in profound ways.

The Within Reach Team is working together to unleash unprecedented compassion on the city. We are tireless about developing next gen leaders to multiply this movement of God to the far corners of the world in business, education, media, church and family life. We are committed to seeing lives transformed by the joy, power and provision of God.

The book in your hands is a collaborative collection of stories from a dozen churches. It is full of lives that are being changed. A bank robber. A business executive. A submarine captain. An intellectual skeptic. A drug addict. A sex addict. An NFL football player. Each one has a story of being changed. We welcome you to an experience of transformation. Hope is within reach. Purpose is within reach. Freedom is within reach. A new beginning is within reach.

Mark Ashton

Senior Editor, Founder, Chairman—Within Reach

1

The Neighbor–
Love Is Within Reach

I was new to the inner city. Unlike my neighbors, I did not grow up with bullet holes in my front door, and I lived with both of my biological parents my entire childhood. I was an outsider coming into a whole new world. I came to North Omaha thinking I would bring change by loving my neighbors. Instead, loving my neighbors changed me.

During my first few months of really investing in the lives of my neighbors, I grew especially close to Kate and Tasha, twin sisters who bounced around from relative to relative. Their ill grandmother was their main caretaker. I had never met their mother or any other family members besides their gang-member brothers. Usually the smell inside the house kept me on the front steps, but today I kept my distance for a different reason. When I opened the broken and stained screen door of the grandmother's 400-square-foot house, I was surprised to greet the girls' mother.

The twins quickly scurried out of the house, excited for a Saturday morning with me. I picked them up on a regular basis to do literally anything—grocery shopping, going to the park, going to church, you name it. That day I could tell they were anxious to leave. The mother, on the other hand, talked up a storm.

"Thank you so much for taking care of my girls. I know they can cause a lot of trouble. I appreciate you spending time with them. I know they love it," she said.

Wearing jeans that were completely unzipped and a ratty t-shirt, she leaned up against the door frame. She reeked of cigarettes and alcohol, and it appeared that she hadn't slept all night. Her bloodshot eyes affirmed my suspicions that she was still drunk from the night before.

"I know my girls. They be gettin' into things. But I don't mind when they go out with you!" she said.

Tasha and Kate were clearly embarrassed. They kept telling their mom that it was time for them to go. Kate tried to zip up her mother's jeans, but her mom just pushed her away.

For fifteen minutes straight the mother continued to thank me, and her daughters continued to try to get her to stop. I didn't want to be rude, but I was uncomfortable with her rambling. But just before we left, she said something I will never forget.

I came to North Omaha thinking I would bring change by loving my neighbors. Instead, loving my neighbors changed me.

"Kate and Tasha, I know they be gettin' into trouble. And I'll ground them from about everything," she said. *"But I will never ground them from going with you... because you are the church!* I want them to be around the church as much as possible. So you're welcome to come over any time you want. I know that when they are with the church, they are in a good place."

Kate and Tasha's mother grasped a concept so many of us miss. Church is not a Sunday morning gathering. It is not a building. Church is a Saturday drive to the park. It's a trip to the grocery store. It's helping with homework. It is simply showing up to be with people. WE are the Church.

Not long after that encounter, I saw clearly how my love for my neighbors impacted not just their mother but the girls.

I was sound asleep one night, when around 2 a.m., I was awakened from what felt like a punch in the gut. *Get up and pray for Tasha and Kate.* I quickly obeyed. I prayed a short prayer and then drifted back to sleep.

The next morning, I didn't think anything of my prayer the night before. I drove to pick up 11-year-old Tasha and Kate like I usually did. Kate ran to me on the sidewalk and greeted me with a big hug and a smile as always.

"Guess what happened last night?" Kate said.

"What?" I asked hesitantly, knowing it probably wasn't going to be good.

"Our house got shot into."

Her facial expression did not match the magnitude of the situation, but mine did. My heart sank into my stomach. I searched her face and her sister's face for more answers. Unsure of what to say, I asked if everyone was okay. I suspected the shooting was probably related to her brothers, who were in a gang.

"Yeah, everyone was okay. Grandma made us all hide in the closet. The bullets ended up in the dresser in the living room. Tasha was crying, but I never cried," Kate said calmly.

"Why didn't you cry?" I asked.

"Well, I know that you were praying for us, so I didn't need to be afraid. I knew we were going to be fine."

That day Kate taught me what faith was. Standing on that sidewalk, I realized that I could no longer sit on the sidelines. I had to get into the game. Too much is at stake for me to not obey God's callings. How many kids are hiding in their closets, terrified? How many windows are being broken from gunshots? How many people need to know someone is on their side? The harvest is plentiful, but the workers are few. The world needs the church—you and me—to be within reach, bringing heaven down to earth.

The names in this story have been changed to protect privacy.

Mary Dotzler is the Director of the Lighthouse Program at ABIDE. She and her husband, Jacob, Ron Dotzler's nephew, are also Lighthouse leaders. Learn more about ABIDE at https://www.abideomaha.org/

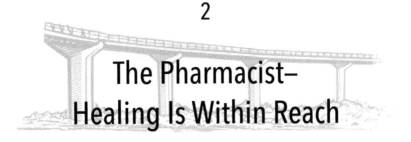

2

The Pharmacist–
Healing Is Within Reach

In his biography of Jesus, his good friend John describes a pool with five porticos, known as the Pool of Bethesda. He tells the story of Jesus' visit to the pool, where he healed a paralytic.

For hundreds of years, skeptics scoffed at the story, saying the pool of Bethseda was not a real place. Nowhere in Jerusalem was there a pool with five porticoes as John reported.

Then, in the 19th Century, archeologists discovered the remains of an ancient pool, right next to the church of St. Anne, just inside the Lion Gate in Jerusalem. This pool had five porticoes, covered by the sands of time. Apparently, John was not making up stories but simply reporting on what he saw and heard.

And we were standing right there—just east of where the pool once served as a gathering place. We were in the place where Jesus once healed a man who could not walk.

I had been leading a trip to Israel with about 45 of my friends from church. In a week's time we visited dozens of places which allowed people to see and walk in places mentioned in the gospels. This stop was unique because we offered to pray for anybody who needed healing: physical, emotional, mental, spiritual...whatever people needed. It seemed particularly appropriate and powerful in this place where Jesus healed centuries ago.

John tells us Jesus asked the man, "Do you want to get well?" So I asked my audience the same thing. It may seem an odd question. Of course they want to get well, right? However, many people become friends with their infirmity and even make it their identity. Before we get well, we must want to get well.

Ron and Jean Baker were among the friends who lined up for prayer. Ron had recently retired from his job as a pharmacist. I had no idea what their maladies might be. But their faith was vibrant—and still is. They both love to follow Jesus and ride in the Christian Motorcycle Association, which gives them the opportunity to reach out to fellow motorcyclists in their cross-country rides.

> *"I danced out of the doctor's office, glad to be healed and glad to not need surgery!"*

They had been anticipating this trip to Israel and were drinking in every minute. They experienced the historical locations where Jesus walked and taught and healed.

Ron told me he had cancer in the tongue. He had "severe dysplasia" and was told that he needed aggressive surgery when he got back from Israel. As soon as he returned from the trip, he would see the doctor to have the cancer removed.

Jean asked for prayer for fibromyalgia. She has struggled for years with multiple symptoms including fatigue, chronic pain, insomnia. My wife, Kelle, and I anointed them with a drop of olive oil, a sign of the presence and power of the Holy Spirit. Then we prayed.

In our straightforward prayers, we expressed faith in God to heal and humble dependence on him for all things.

We prayed with love, with fervency, with expectation. And then, nothing happened.

No tingles, no chills, no rush of power or fainting. In my lifetime, I have prayed over hundreds of people. Most of the time, there is no "special feeling."

On the other hand, I have seen dozens miraculously healed in the moment. I have seen hundreds healed through the God-given skill of doctors and medication. The rest awaited complete healing on the other side of eternity.

Three weeks later, Ron came up to me after church grinning. "Hey Mark, I've got a story for you. I went in for my pre-surgery check." He beamed at me. "The physician's assistant came in and looked at my tongue, then the chart, then my tongue... back and forth. She smiled and left to retrieve the doctor. He did the same thing—looked first at my mouth, then at my chart."

Ron told me that when the doctor finally spoke, his words were shocking. "What I am seeing in your chart is not what I am seeing in your tongue," the doctor told him. "There is nothing serious in there."

"I danced out of the doctor's office, glad to be healed and glad to not need surgery!" Ron's voice grew quiet, though still filled with joy. "Seriously, I am 100 percent healed."

Jean was smiling, as well. I thought she was just happy for Ron. Then she chimed in. "I have a story, too! Inadvertently, I was unable to take my fibromyalgia medication on the flight home. I got home and felt so exhausted I just went to bed without taking it. I woke up pain free so I skipped a dose. I went a few days without it, and I had no symptoms. I just decided to keep the streak going. Still no symptoms. I've gone several weeks symptom free! God has healed me!"

It has been two years since that Israel trip. No return of symptoms. Both Ron and Jean are cured and happy to give the credit to our miracle-working God!

Ron's story was captured by Mark Ashton, senior pastor of Christ Community Church. Learn more about Ron's story and Christ Community at www.cccomaha.org

3

The Foster Parents–
A Loving Family Is Within Reach

Tim Bowes and his wife Jen could both feel something stirring in their hearts. He would often find himself drawn to read James 1:27 over and over: "Religion that God our Father accepts as pure and faultless is this: to look after orphans and widows in their distress and to keep oneself from being polluted by the world."

They sensed God calling them to care for orphans, for the most vulnerable. "It was as if God's desire was jumping out of the Scripture and into my heart," Tim says. "God had laid it on the hearts of my wife and me to care for the most vulnerable in our community."

But what would that look like? They began to learn about foster care.

"It was hard to wrap our minds around the child welfare system and how circumstances could come to a point where a child is removed from their family and placed into another home. After talking with other foster families, doing some research, and having a discussion with our three school-aged children, my wife and I agreed that it was God's desire for us to become a licensed foster family."

Tim and Jen went through excellent training, but they say that no training can prepare you for the real stories of children whose lives are so desperate they need to be taken from their parents for their own safety.

"Our first foster child was with us for about nine months," Tim recalls. "He was born of a man with eight children by six women. Our foster son's mother was a prostitute."

Baby Robert had severe medical issues. He passed away on the Valentine's Day before his second birthday.

"I loved baby Robert, but in my heart I had hatred toward his parents," Tim admits. "In my grief after his death, God graciously showed me his heart. God revealed that his love for baby Robert's parents was the same as his love for me. His love is endless and pure. In this revelation, God changed my heart and opened my eyes."

Tim and his family continued to foster children, who stay anywhere from a few days to several months.

"There was always a bit of uncertainty with what would happen during each stay. How would the kids fit in with the family? How long would they stay? What have they been through that brought them to us? Regardless of who they were or the circumstances that brought them here, we tried to remain true to our calling to open our home and love them as best we can while they stay with us."

Eventually, Tim and his wife realized their season as a foster family was ending. They adopted three children from foster care and became one forever family, thus changing their family tree forever.

Because they already had six children, the state would not allow the Bowes to receive any more foster children in the home and, eventually, their foster care license expired.

"We were at peace with that since our time was consumed with caring for our three school-aged kids and three new additions who were all under two years of age," Tim says. "While we were no longer a licensed foster care home, we knew that we were not done with the foster care system. It was not until about seven years later when our kids were older that God began to stir our hearts and show us his plan."

Tim kept asking himself about the role of the church in the foster care system. He came across an organization called Live the Promise in Atlanta. They had built a ministry based on the premise that if every church in Atlanta had at least one foster family, then there would be enough safe, Christian homes for every foster child.

Additionally, Tim explains, Live the Promise builds a Care Team to surround and support each foster family, so they are not alone. A Care Team is a group of six to eight people who play specific roles that support a foster family in practical, tangible ways.

Care Team members can consist of anyone willing to serve—family, friends, church members or neighbors. A typical Care Team provides one meal each week for a foster family. Care Team members are encouraged to stay and eat with the foster family to build relationship with the foster child.

A Care Team might provide a few hours of respite once or twice a month so that the foster parents can take a break. Care Teams have done yard work, cleaned houses, shoveled snow, provided transportation and many other practical helps. Care Teams also pray—daily!

All of this is coordinated in an online calendar put together by the Care Team Leader with feedback from the foster family. With the support of the church and active engagement of Care Teams, families are fostering longer and stronger.

"We feel like our role is to be a voice for foster families and biological families to surround them with a tangible expression of God's love."

"Now, we feel like our role is to be a voice for foster families and biological families to surround them with a tangible expression of God's love," Tim says. "We believe it is God's desire for foster families to thrive and not just survive. With an understanding of God's heart for the most vulnerable in our community, with support from a few local churches and with a response of people who have heard and understood God's calling, Jen and I have launched Care Teams in our community with a hope of surrounding every foster family with a Care Team backed by the support of the local church.

"We love Care Teams so much because it embraces everything that God has taught us," Tim says. "Some people are ready to foster, some are prayer warriors, some can provide a meal and some want to mentor. God has taught us to meet people where they are at. The beauty of Care Teams lies in the fact that everyone can reach the broken through the calling and giftings that God has given them."

To date, Tim and Jen have established eight Care Teams through five local churches in Omaha. This support has transformed the lives of foster families and foster children.

"The feedback we receive has been a tremendous blessing and encouragement for us to continue to seek out foster families that want support and churches that are willing to be a part of the process," Tim says. "We are grateful for the journey which God has given us to foster, adopt and bring transformation to our community."

Tim's story was captured by Rafael Aristy, Executive Pastor of Good News Church, where Jason Carter is Lead Pastor. For more information about the story or this church, go to goodnews.church

4

The Abuse Survivor– Reconciliation Is Within Reach

Like many people who grow up in a broken home, Monica's life replayed the patterns of abuse and addiction. Until she finally found the God who is within reach.

Monica's parents divorced when she was just two years old. When she went to live with her mother in Germany, she was separated from her father and brother in the States. She remembers incidents of sexual abuse from her childhood, beginning when she was only six years old.

As an adult, Monica carried her wounds with her. She was married three times, each time to men who did not treat her well. During her first two marriages, she was blessed with four children who are the apple of her eye.

While married to her second husband, Monica crashed her car, landed in a 30-foot deep ravine and was thrown through the windshield.

I visited her at the trauma ward and prayed with her. Miraculously, she survived!

Despite this incredible sparing of her life, she continued to make choices that led to pain. While she was married to her third husband, Monica began intravenously using meth. After a year of committing a series of crimes across two states, she and her husband were finally arrested in Lincoln, Nebraska.

Child Protective Services took her children and sent them to live with her brother. She stayed with her abusive husband. Monica's sole focus at this point was to get her children back. Her husband told her he loved her and promised to change. Monica, not knowing the love of God or the healthy love of a father, believed him—again and again. She covered up the abuse because she knew the state wouldn't grant her custody if she lived in an abusive home.

Monica continued in this abusive marriage for several more years, until her husband attacked and almost strangled her to death. He went to jail. Monica had hit rock bottom because all hope of regaining custody of her children was gone. She was all alone. She was a broken shell of the person God had created her to be. Her personality was gone. Kids gone. No hope. No joy. No peace. She felt lifeless.

Of course, she wasn't really alone. Jesus was with her. Holocaust survivor Corrie ten Boom famously said, "There is no pit so deep God's love is not deeper still." No matter how deep and wide a mess our life has become, God is waiting for us to say yes to his unfathomable, relentless love. It is when we accept God's love, even at our worst, that the healing can begin.

Monica's brother, who had custody of her children, gave her the name of a church and encouraged her to go there. Previously she had resisted, but, after about two weeks of hearing God's voice telling her to go, she relented and finally went to church. The slow but steady process of healing began.

I met with her brother several times, crying with him as we prayed for reconciliation. We prayed for him to forgive her and allow God to redeem her and her family.

At church, Monica heard of the unchanging love of God and was welcomed into a loving community. She began to walk the many steps of the process towards healing. It didn't come overnight. Monica continued to visit her husband in jail every day, despite the fact he had strangled her. Her friends at church encouraged her to leave him, but Monica didn't have the strength to put an end to the relationship. Finally, two months before his release from prison, with the support from her new friends from church and her beautiful relationship with Jesus, she had the strength to end her unhealthy marriage and release the toxic relationship.

As Monica continued to heal, the Lord spoke the word "believe" to her. She saw this word everywhere, and it impacted her heart every time. The Lord was calling her to believe and trust in Him, a difficult thing considering all the abuse she had endured. One day she was crying out to God to help her get her kids back. Even as a Christian, she had been trying to beg, connive and manipulate to get her kids back. But on that day, she finally just let go. She surrendered the entire situation to God. She finally gave up all her attempts to control and turned everything over to God, including her children. Monica recalls that seconds after her releasing it all to God her phone rang with the news she was getting her kids back on Sunday!

Monica has now been reunited with her children for several years and is the proud grandmother of four grandchildren. Monica is continually amazed at the healing God has worked in her life and in her family since the day she turned to Him. She smiles at the future and knows God has plans to continue the healing process as she deepens her relationship with Jesus, the Lover of her soul.

Monica's story was captured by Walter Hooker, Senior Associate Pastor of Bellevue Christian Center. For more information about the story or this church, go to www.bellevuechristian.com

5

The Bank Robber–
Reform Is Within Reach

I couldn't believe it. Literally, I couldn't believe it. I'd heard a lot of stories from well-meaning people seeking attention or assistance, but this was one of the biggest. I had to call his pastor, my friend Marty, to confirm the tale because it was all so improbable.

He told me that he had just gotten out of jail for robbing banks. Five of them. Shon Hopwood is his name, and he appeared to be in his late twenties. Crazy thing. He was from David City, Nebraska, a sleepy rural farm town where nothing exciting ever happened. And that was exactly the problem. He was bored. Not starving or deprived—just bored.

He had gone to college on a basketball scholarship but dropped out due to academics. He worked odd jobs around town, but none of them satisfied his sense of adventure.

So he and his friends cooked up plans to rob banks and live on the run. And their plan worked… the first time. And the second, third and fourth. But the fifth time, they got sloppy and eventually got caught. Only in his early twenties, Shon was sentenced to twelve years in federal prison.

Sitting across from me in the office, he was totally unassuming. Shon was tall and athletic—built for basketball. His dark hair was parted on the side, and his smile was contagious. He spoke at a slow, deliberate pace and did not seem like he was exaggerating. He had a penchant for precision. And yet the stories were way too much.

I listened for a long time before I asked far too many questions. He told me stories of being in prison with guys who were tough criminals. He talked about other guys who were just in on small-time drug charges, but got the shaft because of bad lawyers or harsh minimum sentencing laws. Shon spent his time in prison earning respect on the basketball court. He read books that were sent to him by his hometown pastor, Marty Barnhart. He developed a deep romantic pen pal relationship with his hometown heartthrob, Ann Marie. And he studied law to see if there was any way out of the bars and barbed wire.

Nobody wants to go to prison. And when you get there, it is worse than you thought. So you do what it takes to survive, and you do what it takes to get out. Shon thought there might be some legal technicalities or loopholes in his case, but the truth was, they had him dead to rights. He was guilty.

But while he searched for loopholes, he found that he loved the law. Especially supreme court law. Shon got a job in the law library and began to read voraciously. After all, what else is there to do in prison? His bent for logic and precision served him well. At the same time, he studied about Jesus. Marty sent him books that were filled with legal-style evidence for the life and teachings of Jesus. Shon found them compelling and asked for more.

In all of his legal and spiritual studies, two things became clear. The case for Jesus became increasingly clear. Dozens of prophecies pointed to him. The evidence for his historical life, death and even resurrection were abundantly clear. The empty tomb, the live appearances, the changed lives, the world movement. Who could deny that Jesus was real? The case for Shon's imprisonment also was clear. No loopholes or technicalities.

But Shon listened to one of his fellow prisoners—John. His conviction was muddy. In fact, it became evident that John had gotten the shaft. A lethal combination of bad circumstances and incompetent representation landed him in a federal prison in Illinois. It put Shon's passion juices on high. He went to the library and immersed himself in constitutional law. He had to know it inside and out. Shon believed that his friend's conviction actually violated the constitution.

Shon not only learned the subtleties of the constitution, he also learned the precedents of related law and how to write a supreme court brief—because he was going to try, from inside a prison cell, to advocate for his fellow cell mate. Every term had to be used properly. The format had to be exacting. He used a typewriter because computers weren't available. He prayed to Jesus because he knew that an average of 7,000-8,000 briefs would be sent to the Supreme Court in a term, and only 80 would be accepted. Almost all were composed by trained lawyers specializing in supreme court law. His argument was subtle but sensible. After reviewing every detail possible, he typed it and sent it. Oh, the audacity! Even if it never made it past a law clerk, at least working on it helped pass the time in prison.

Shon – from prison – had not one, but TWO Supreme Court briefs approved and cases won!

For months he waited. One day, when he was headed to the recreation yard, a friend of his came running out of the housing unit, screaming. He carried a newspaper in his hand. The friend had a copy of *USA Today,* which had an article saying that John's case had been granted by the U.S. Supreme Court and how unlikely that was, given John had filed without a lawyer.

Of course Shon could not advocate from prison and, truth be told, that would have been a horrible idea. So Seth Waxman, an experienced veteran of the court, took over the case. He took it on one condition—that he would have full access to consult with Shon Hopwood. After all, Shon knew the case backward and forward. He knew the law. He was a critical piece. And so, Shon got a mentor.

Seth argued the case and won unanimously! When John was released early, Shon had a deep sense of gratitude... and accomplishment.

But wait! The story becomes even more fantastic. Because lightning struck twice. Another cellmate. Another constitutional issue. Another brief. Another win. Shon—from prison—had, not one, but two Supreme Court briefs approved and cases won!

When Shon was released from prison early, by law he had to live in Omaha, Nebraska, while on supervised release. When I met him at Christ Community Church, he was looking for a job. He had just discovered there are three cities in all of the United States that have publishers who formally prepare Supreme Court briefs. Of all the cities in America, Omaha is one. Shon applied for an administrative role in copying and binding documents. As a former bank robber and ex-con, he was happy to have any job. Imagine the surprise of the employer when Shon told his story. He had to check references on this one! After confirming with Seth Waxman, Shon was hired to consult with lawyers about their briefs.

It was an incredible joy to see Shon and his new bride, Annie, grow in their faith at Christ Community Church. For three years, they lived in Omaha, loved each other, had children (their oldest is named Mark!) and grew in their faith. Of course, Shon dreamed of bigger things when he finished his supervised release. He dreamt of law school—and of specializing in constitutional law. An ex-con is not allowed to try a case before the Supreme Court, but Shon hoped he could find a niche somewhere.

I remember when the big moment came. "Against all odds, I got in!" he said. "And they gave me a big fat scholarship! I am going to the University of Washington. Thanks so much for your investment in me. I sure hope I can use my life to make a difference."

As of the writing of this book, Shon has graduated from the University of Washington Law School, is married to Annie, the girl of his dreams, has two kids and is a law professor at Georgetown University Law Center. His is a passionate advocate for prison reform. His full story can be found in his autobiography, Law Man: Memoir of a Jailhouse Lawyer.

This story was gathered by Mark Ashton, Lead Pastor of Christ Community Church. For more information, or to get in contact with Shon, email info@cccomaha.org

6

The Juvenile Delinquent—
Change Is Within Reach

I grew up in New York City's Lower East Side, raised by a single mom who loved me and did the best she knew how. But I often felt isolated and alone, disconnected from everyone and everything around me. When I was 16, I got into trouble with the law when I sold heroin to an undercover cop. In case you ever wonder—that's never a good idea. The judge sentenced me to 18 months of incarceration and five years of probation, served concurrently.

By God's grace, the judge gave me the opportunity to serve my sentence at Boys Town, a residential community for troubled youth in Omaha, Nebraska.

When I first heard the possibility of serving my sentence in Nebraska, I yelled, "Alaska! I don't want to go to Alaska!"

"No, NEB-raska. Not Alaska. Nebraska."

"Is that a state?" I asked. (Don't judge me. I had to repeat second grade twice.)

Eventually I boarded a plane and headed to Boys Town. Little did I know God took me halfway across the country—away from everything familiar—so I could hear him for the first time.

Nebraska felt like a different planet. There were so many white people, I thought I got selected for a part in a movie. When I got asked to mow the lawn for the first time, my response didn't go so well. But mostly, I had trouble sleeping because the whole place was so quiet.

While many of the cares and concerns I carried in NYC were gone, I continued to feel isolated and alone. I excelled in the home and the classroom. I was even called a "role model," but the angst never left. I tried everything to meet the deepest needs of my soul. I lived recklessly; I lived self-righteously. Neither worked.

Six months after my arrival at Boys Town, my younger brother landed in Nebraska. New York rejoiced to be rid of him, too. He landed in a home with a young couple, Bobby and Rhonda Betzold. I dubbed Bobby "Jesus T-shirt guy." You know, that guy who only owns clothing screen-printed with Bible verses. That was Bobby.

Bobby and Rhonda shared their faith in Jesus, and my brother began asking questions. Then my little brother began telling me about the hope he found in Jesus. Something had changed.

For the first time in my life I had a conversation with God. "God, I want what my brother has. If it means Jesus, then that's what I want."

Honestly, the whole thing freaked me out. "Those white people brainwashed you!" I tried to convince him, but what he had to say about Jesus intrigued me. My heart longed for what he seemed to have.

My brother was different. I couldn't deny the change. He was still himself, but different. Real joy and freedom loosed the grip of deep anger and "psycho-ness." But mostly, my brother possessed a confidence I lacked. He knew what God thought of him and where he stood with God. Unlike me, he didn't seem isolated and alone.

I wanted that same sense of belonging. But pride kept me from admitting my desire.

One day, my brother visited my house and began sharing about Jesus. Irritated and angry, I kicked him out. "If you wanna come over to hang out, cool, but don't come to preach at me."

His eyes filled with tears, shocking me. My brother was genuinely hurt.

"Fine. If you don't believe me, read it for yourself." He tossed his Bible on my bed.

And he left.

"IF YOU DON'T BELIEVE ME, READ IT FOR YOURSELF!"

I couldn't shake those words. So I decided to take up his challenge.

Over the next few days, I read the Bible, randomly choosing 2 Corinthians in the New Testament. Five chapters in, something happened. It sounds cliché, but I literally felt a light bulb go off in my mind. The verse read: "If anyone is in Christ, he is a new creation. The old has gone, and the new has come!"

BOOM! That explained what happened to my brother. He became a new creation.

I remember the day vividly. I can still picture lying on my bed with the Bible on my chest. For the first time in my life, I had a conversation with God.

"God, I want what my brother has. If it means Jesus, then that's what I want."

Something changed in me that night. For the first time ever, I no longer felt isolated and alone. I couldn't stop reading. The more I heard from God through his Word, the more he continued to change me.

He's still changing me through his Word.

Reading the Word (Bible) allowed me to encounter Jesus. The real Jesus. Not cultural Jesus. Not Jesus as I want him to be, but Jesus as he is.

I can turn Jesus into my homeboy. Friendly, but not fierce. I can turn him into a distant relative I love, but don't think about often and who doesn't really impact my day-to-day life. I can turn Jesus into a political activist who is the champion of whatever cause I feel strongly about at that given moment. I can turn Jesus into whatever I want.

But when I spend time in God's Word, he simply won't let me.

God's Word revealed so much to me: Jesus who changed me when he made me a new creation (2 Cor 5:17); Jesus who is the fulfillment of all of God's promises (1 Cor 1:20); Jesus who both washes me of the stain on my soul and invites me to be with him (John 13) and so much more!

Jesus conquered the foe I could not. When I had served my sentence, I came out of Boys Town changed. The Jesus I needed when I was 17 and the Jesus I need today—as a husband, father, pastor, and friend—has changed my life, and continues to change it. He is within reach, no matter where life takes me.

Elvin Torres serves as Pastor of New City Church in Bellevue, Nebraska. For information about this story or New City, visit http://www.newcityomaha.org

7

The Lawyer–
New Identity Is Within Reach

I'm half Jewish, half Marine, and the middle child. My older sister was a genius. She had nearly perfect scores on her college entrance exams and was class valedictorian. My younger sister was even smarter than my older sister. She scored not only higher on her exams, she was also the valedictorian, a national merit scholar, and a beauty pageant finalist. As for me, I was neither valedictorian nor a beauty pageant finalist. One day, after taking a long look, my grandma told me, "At least you've got a good personality." My mom confided in me recently that she believed my mouth would either make me money or get me into trouble. As a lawyer, both turned out to be true.

My dad, the Marine, kept military time and did a "pre-flight checklist" for everything. My mom, a businesswoman, was the daughter of an Ashkenazic Jew and Lutheran nurse. She lived in Germany as a child. Her father, an attorney for the United States Army, prosecuted Nazis during the Nuremberg War Crimes Trials. My mom's brother, my uncle, became my state's attorney general, then a four-term governor, and finally, a U.S. Congressman. When he died, a rabbi blew the shofar for the first and likely only time ever inside a Lutheran church. With one-half of the family Jewish and the other half Christian, holiday dinners included spirited debates about religion, politics, and which dishes were pork-free for the practicing Jews and sugar-free for the practicing diabetics.

As an adult, I didn't fit any mold. Neither Jewish nor Christian, I left home and began to search for myself. I wandered, traveled, and lingered. I can't recall what happened first—the hurt or the addiction. But along the way I got hurt, and along the way I became addicted. While the order is irrelevant, the effect was perpetual and self-sustaining. I lived on the very edge of life for a long time. I stopped sleeping at night. I couldn't breathe in the dark. I couldn't breathe in the light. Fear poured over me like an incessant waterfall. I was sure I was dying. I *was* dying.

Five days after my husband and I bought a house, I collapsed to the ground while pulling up the old carpet in the dining room. In that moment, I knew I was as far from God as anyone had ever been. I was carried out of our house by stretcher and loaded into an ambulance. My diagnosis: low oxygen levels. Tests to follow.

I returned home in despair, and found a Bible stashed in my closet. I opened it and started to read. For the first time in years, I could breathe. We randomly picked a church to attend, whose sermon that week happened to be, "Let God Be Your Oxygen." We went back the next Sunday, my husband still drunk from the night before. A stranger sitting behind him rubbed his back. We went home and poured out all the alcohol.

With nothing to lose, we kept going back to church. One night, right in the middle of an evening sermon, I started weeping and couldn't stop. I got out of my seat and laid myself down at the foot of a big old cross standing in the corner. I wept through the service. I wept after the service. I wept as I walked to my car. And I wept as I drove home. I was so utterly and horrifically broken, I finally surrendered my life to the Lord Jesus Christ, even though I had no idea who he was. I desperately needed a Savior. In the next few weeks, I went on to answer numerous altar calls—just to make *sure* I was saved and forgiven. It was hard to believe.

Slowly, very slowly, I walked out of darkness and addiction and fear. I looked for God and found him in the Old Testament. The night before I was to give oral arguments to a large audience, I fell asleep drowning in fear once again. In the middle of the night, I awoke to the words *Jeremiah 1:9* repeated over and over in my mind. I had no idea what they were. I turned on the light and opened my Bible to Jeremiah 1:9: "Then the LORD reached out his hand and touched my mouth and said to me, 'I have put my words in your mouth.'"

As I began to embrace my new identity in Christ, I started to wear my necklace that combined the Star of David with a cross. One day, my husband and I took a homeless man out to eat. That afternoon, a page from someone's devotional blew into our yard. It said that when you feed the hungry, you serve Christ. Later, even though we didn't have any money, I made an internal commitment to the Lord to tithe. The very day I was to transfer funds to begin payment on an $8,000 student loan, I received written notice from the lender the debt had been cancelled.

But God wasn't always in the thunder, so I started to wrestle with him, like Jacob. I would beg him to remove obstacles, which he did not always remove. I would cry out to Jesus but could not always hear or understand him. I would go on long midnight runs—mile after mile—and ask to feel his presence, which I did not always feel. At times I thought I might even lose my faith, it was so weak. But I didn't. For the last sixteen years, my understanding and faith in Jesus has grown only as I have walked through the valleys of doubt and despair. For not only does he understand, he fights for me. And notwithstanding me, he remains steadfast—even on the midnight run. I don't have to see anymore, I finally know.

Aimee's story was captured by Mike Hintz of Lifegate Church, where Les Beauchamp is the Senior Pastor. For more information about the story or Lifegate, visit www.discoverlifegate.com

8

The Meth Addict–
Sobriety Is Within Reach

Being a shy redhead, I was tormented at school. In junior high I was constantly afraid of being beat up, so I started to carry knives for security. I thought that would protect me, but instead, I developed a reputation for being dangerous. In high school, I found friends who were drug users, so I acted like one, too. And then I became one. It felt good to be part of a group of people who accepted me.

Even though partying and my friends always came first, I met a girl who was loving and responsible. All I wanted to do was party all night and sleep all day. Brenda worked, paid rent and took care of the house and me. She was used to taking care of children, and I was used to being one.

All I remember about our wedding day is running home to get high. We had a son right away. I was so proud, but I remember having to leave the hospital to go find drugs. Using crystal meth gave me energy for days with no need of sleep, but then I would sleep 20 hours to recover. Crystal meth was a rocket ride to the bottom. Normal men want sex often, but crystal meth addicts want it all the time. Meth addicts wear out a spouse. My wife felt the shame of being used, while I was never satisfied. When I would try to stop using, I turned into a monster I couldn't control.

Thinking it was for financial reasons, I agreed to a divorce. It's hard to describe that portion of my life. All I knew was rage, and I missed my son desperately. I begged my wife to take me back. I tried to make her feel ashamed and guilty for tearing me away from my son, but she was strong in her faith, and God told her she had to let me go.

I became a danger to my son. When he was five, he playfully hit me in the face, and in an instant of uncontrollable rage, I hit him back. I had no self-control. I scared myself so much I knew only one way left to keep my family safe. I had to die.

I remember looking through the phone book for the suicide prevention hotline or the phone number for that egg in the frying pan commercial. The one that says, "This is your brain on drugs." I found myself at a counseling center, but I left quickly because I had severe anxiety when I was around people.

That Christmas my son had the flu, and I was absolutely no help to him. I hid in my bedroom while everyone else did Christmas. I still see him in my memory, sitting by himself. It is one of my saddest memories.

All I remember about our wedding day is running home to get high. We had a son right away. I was so proud, but I remember having to leave the hospital to go find drugs.

I went back to the counselor determined to do what I was told. She gave me a pamphlet about Alcoholics Anonymous meetings. That night I was dying inside, and I took out the booklet wondering why I had a booklet for alcoholism when I didn't drink much. The next meeting—at 4:30 a.m.—was nicknamed sleepwalkers, and that's what I felt like. I showed up at the meeting, and a guy told his story a story of addiction and desperation. After that, I started to go to meetings three times a day.

It was so hard and painful in the beginning. I saw my counselor twice a week, and I rode my bike to get to meetings. The first step in Alcoholics Anonymous' Twelve Steps is accepting that I am powerless over drugs and that addiction made my life unmanageable. I had no problem with that step. It was the truth, and I could see it. The second step was believing a power greater than ourselves could restore us to sanity. I knew I was insane, but I didn't believe in a greater power.

Even harder, step three was to turn my life over to God. But I didn't believe God existed. However, I believed in evil, and drugs were evil, so I realized I had to find God or die. This made me desperate enough to go to church.

The sermon that first Sunday was about the love of God, and how Satan wanted to tear me apart. I knew that feeling. Something inside me broke for good. I knew I was sick and could be healed from guilt and shame and the monster that was me.

I found someone I could trust in Jesus. I found my mentor. I found my God. I started to love. My heart broke for what I had put my wife through. I felt a new love for her that made me pray daily she would find somebody who would love her like she deserved—even if it wasn't me. I devoted my life to serving her and my son by shoveling snow, fixing things around her house and helping out however I could. She was confused, but we started to communicate on a real level. God showed me how to care for her and be interested in her and others.

I started to become a father in the simplest ways I knew how. I took my son to movies and learned to talk to him between the movies and commercials. Slowly, I became closer with Brenda and my son. Even though she was scared, we renewed our relationship. I understood why she was scared, but I was no longer the man she had known. He was dead and buried. I didn't know it, but I had become the man I was praying for her to have.

Eventually, Brenda and I remarried. When she was walking down the aisle, I wondered if she would turn around and run away. But she didn't, and I learned the new life of being a godly father and husband. It was like growing up all over again in a right and better way. Today, the word love seems too small to express all that God has taught me.

Darren's story was captured by Mike Hintz of Lifegate Church, where Les Beauchamp is the Senior Pastor. For more information about the story or Lifegate, visit www.discoverlifegate.com

9

The Submarine Captain– Reorientation Is Within Reach

We ate the best broasted chicken in Omaha at the Millard Roadhouse as he regaled me with story after story of his life in submarines. Jim had spent over 12 years of his life on sea duty—four of them under the polar icecap. His stories came from a world I knew nothing about: a hundred men crammed in a sardine can powered by a nuclear reactor surrounded by high voltage, explosives and sea water. What could possibly go wrong?

Jim had always been an all-star; he graduated with honors from the Naval Academy as a marine engineer. He was selected for the Naval Nuclear Propulsion Program and submarines where he served on a Trident "Boomer" and three "attack boats." The men on the sub loved Jim, and he took quickly to leadership roles, learning some hard lessons by trial and error. There was little room for compassion. You got things done or were quickly eliminated. His engineering mind and great decision-making were the perfect combo for military leadership. While at the Naval Academy, he met Tammy on a blind date, fell in love and married her after graduation. Neither Jim nor Tammy followed Jesus.

Jim was the consummate workaholic. The Cold War operations tempo was high, and Jim would often disappear for months on end. Separation from Tammy and his two kids was so normal that on one occasion he forgot to tell Tammy that he was going to sea for three days. Tammy was married, but she lived like a single mom.

As a result of his hard work, Jim was promoted to the rank of commander and given his own submarine to command. Imagine the awesome responsibility of being commissioned to own the depths of the ocean, carrying a variety of weapons and sensors, with Cold War politics making war possible at any moment. It was a challenge to lead a crew of rowdy, sleep-deprived 20-something sailors confined and isolated from the world inside a steel tube. His focus was on the mission and keeping his charges in line.

Jim wasn't hostile toward God, but science and engineering gave him adequate explanation for everything in the world—especially his world. So he had himself and didn't need God. Life at home seemed good, and he was climbing the ladder of success.

Jim was the last commander of the USS Phoenix (SSN 702) before it was decommissioned. So respected was his leadership that he was promoted to the rank of captain and assigned as the commanding officer of Submarine Base New London in Groton, Connecticut. Jim and Tammy thrived in this role, as people both respected by their track record and loved for their caring nature.

Omaha is not on the list of places a submariner wants to live, but in the military you move toward your next promotion or you are moved out. The Navy tapped Jim on the shoulder and asked him to move to Omaha to be director of operations for the USSTRATCOM Joint Force Component Command, Space and Global Strike. The role was intense, but through common sense, great communication, years of experience and 80+ hour work-weeks, Jim rose to the occasion and led with excellence.

At the same time as success was dramatic in his career, there was something hollow on the inside. Jim's marriage was falling apart. He felt dissatisfied. His sense of purpose was waning. He was exhausted and looking for something bigger and more exciting to fill the void.

A friend who was a local beekeeper invited Jim to his acreage to check out the bees. Jim's voracious appetite for learning brought him to study the little creatures. The way they were able to create honey. The little dances they did for each other to communicate. But the biggest marvel of all was the hive. It was made up of perfect little hexagonal segments. Each was the perfect size and perfect structure. Not only did it protect the bees and hold the honey, but it was structurally PERFECT. Only the most brilliant of architects could plan this in all of its simplicity, beauty and power.

Now a bee's brain is not that big. And without the hive and honey and queen, a bee could not survive. Somehow bees thrived without training, without assistance. In September of 2012, Jim found himself thinking that there must be an architect, an engineer, a designer behind it all. God spoke to Jim. For the first time in

At the same time as success was dramatic in his career, there was something hollow on the inside. Jim's marriage was falling apart. He felt dissatisfied.

decades, Jim had a powerful sense that there is a God—the greatest engineer ever—and he developed the bees, the honeycomb and everything else.

At the same time, Jim's wife, Tammy, got an urge. An urge to go to church. She saw the big Christ Community Church sign and steeple on the side of the road and knew that she needed to stop by. Her life, their marriage, felt stalled out. Maybe God could get things back on track. They showed up on a Sunday morning, with some apprehension about this foreign culture of singing and hugs and teaching from an ancient book. God was waiting for them.

The message that morning was from Ruth, a love story about Ruth and Boaz that represented the powerful love of God for broken and hurting and empty people. They heard that God takes people who are in a mess and makes them beautiful and wanted. Jim and Tammy knew they had to come back for more. God told Jim that morning that he was in the business of second chances.

Two months later on Easter Sunday, every member of the congregation received a flattened box. Jim, the engineer, folded it into three dimensions almost immediately. The message was about how often we keep God in a box—hidden in our basement, safe and under control—and how we need to let God out of the box to have a wise ruler in our lives. Jim and Tammy reflected on their lives. They knew boxes. In 20 military moves, they sometimes would not get around to unpacking before they had to move again. The boxes just stayed in the basement unopened. And this was where they had placed God 37 years earlier.

That morning, Jim opened the box, and Jesus met him. He trusted the ultimate engineer with the powerful love story. God has created a revolution in Jim's life. Today, Jim and Tammy passionately follow Jesus. Their marriage and family have been fully restored and considered to be not only life-giving, but triumphant. Today, they love to tell their story of transformation and new life with Jesus and invite others to open the box.

Jim left his consulting gig with the military and pursued a masters degree in Christian Leadership. Not long later, he pursued licensing as a pastor and was eventually ordained at that church along the interstate with the big steeple, where he currently serves as an executive pastor. And it started with bees, a box and a big God.

This story was gathered by Mark Ashton, the lead pastor of Christ Community Church. For more information about the church or to meet Jim, Tammy, or the bees, contact info@cccomaha.org.

10

The Overachiever– Grace Is Within Reach

My three-year-old feet, donned with white ruffled socks and patent leather shoes, dangled from the large oak bench in the cavernous courthouse. Heels clicked down the corridor, echoing in my ears. Confused and afraid, I waited outside the courtroom as my parents ended their marriage. I felt small and insignificant as they negotiated custody arrangements.

The bang of the gavel labeled me with a new identity. My brother and I became the first children with divorced parents at our elementary school in South Dakota. We lived with my mom and stepfather, while my dad came to visit us every Tuesday and Thursday. Every other weekend, we stayed with my dad.

I know my parents loved me very much, but my childhood lacked security. Living amidst emotional chaos, shuffling back and forth between homes and trying to understand complex situations and feelings challenged me. To cope, I learned self-preservation tactics—all in an attempt to earn love. I believed I would experience stability and emotional peace *only if* I got good grades, avoided trouble and became the *best* at everything.

Escape came through involvement in school and extracurricular activities— student body president, homecoming queen, newspaper editor, president of youth group and a member of the tennis, basketball and softball teams. I even created a youth mentoring program called Kids for Kids.

I didn't realize that every activity and every accomplishment was an attempt to earn love and approval. The enemy rooted these positive activities in what would become a 30-year performance addiction.

I believed in Jesus, and knew I wasn't alone; however, deep down my strongest desire was not for Him, but for approval. Serving in youth group, reading my Bible, seeking God's presence—I *did* all these things, confusing the approval of others for love.

I accepted a scholarship for the Chancellor's Leadership Program at the University of Nebraska-Lincoln, where I pursued a degree in communications. My future looked bright as I left my challenging childhood behind to begin life anew. I thought going to college would free me, allow me to start over.

Unaware of my performance addiction and the foothold the enemy had on me, I tapped every available opportunity to shine. After all, my new horizon came with more chances to prove myself to more people. A bigger playing field meant better possibilities to perform.

Sorority rush chair, student ambassador, homecoming court, speechwriter for the governor and lieutenant governor, proposal writer for large donors of Campaign Nebraska, volunteer coordinator at the University's Women's Center—my accomplishments fed my performance addiction.

I attended church and read my Bible daily, but I lived a double life. I dated an atheist and made too many unhealthy choices. Like the lyrics to a popular country song, I looked for love and acceptance in all the wrong places.

At age 23, I became an entrepreneur (as others in my family had done for generations); I began a business with a multi-billion-dollar direct-selling company. I was sold on the promise of freedom, flexibility, independence, unlimited income and advancement. The new opportunity to earn approval came veiled in a beautiful package: the illusion of financial freedom.

How blind I was to the trap of scoreboard-based performance.

The sales and commission scoreboard monitored hourly, daily, weekly, monthly and yearly production at work. Often fickle, the scoreboard reflected effort and sacrifice one moment, but not the next. It ascribed value to people based on their performance or lack thereof. Accolades, recognition and fame came at the price of more pressure and unrealistic expectations.

I mastered the game, worked the time frames and used my skill set to get results. Every win became a *fix* for me, no different than a hit of cocaine for a drug addict.

> *I didn't realize that every activity, every accomplishment, was an attempt to earn love and approval. The enemy rooted these positive activities in what would become a 30-year performance addiction.*

Reaching key milestones on the success track resulted in increased income and perks; however, I experienced only momentary satisfaction. After all, the scoreboard never stopped counting. Winning simply meant another goal waited for me.

Each success fed my ego, insecurities, inflated self-importance, vanity, perfectionism and workaholism. The impact carried over to my family. My husband and two daughters suffered from my relentless schedule, the pressure to appear perfect and unhealthy lifestyle expectations. They sacrificed, navigating my weariness, erratic moods, anxiety and absences. They accepted my *leftovers* and embraced me with love and support.

The intensity of this environment slowly suffocated me.

I masked my internal struggles. I taught Bible studies, led small groups, hosted weekend retreats, held prayer calls, spoke from stages to thousands of people and led people to Christ. Still, I could not shake the focus on performance: *doi*ng for Christ versus *being* in Christ.

I reached the pinnacle position in the company at age 37. My future was set—executive income, luxury cars, international vacations, speaking engagements around the world, a retirement plan and more.

The downside? The perks and comforts came with shackles. *Enough* was never *enough*. The enemy had come to lie, steal, kill, destroy—and enslave me. After all, there was always *more* to be earned and achieved, the next sales contest to win. My performance addiction hijacked everything—my self-value, my perceptions, my choices, my schedule, my marriage and my family.

I was dying a slow death.

Bondage to work had taken its toll. I could no longer keep up with the demands of the game. Sucked into the worldly current of *more, more, more,* I hardly recognized the person I'd become after 20 years. My entire identity was misaligned from God's true purposes for my life.

Graciously, Jesus *divinely disorientated* me and began removing scales from my eyes, reminding me that only his love, which never has to be earned, fulfills and sets us free.

Fully surrendering my plans, success and control was difficult. I feared disappointing people and losing relationships. I even attempted to negotiate with God, hoping to straddle the fence.

Clearly, this was not what God had in mind. I had to choose to obey or disobey. I chose surrender, praying, "Lord, remove anything in me not of you, and replace it with something I'd be willing to die for."

He responded, "Your current assignment is finished. I have given you something to die for—Me and My Kingdom."

Jesus gave me confidence to walk away from the career track which enslaved me, to freely pursue his ultimate love and purposes. Through him and him alone, I summoned the courage to *unfollow* MY plans in order to *follow* HIS perfect dreams for me.

I'm so grateful to have a Savior who loves us despite our brokenness, weaknesses and flaws. I know this to be true: all the promotions, wins, money, performance, perks and privileges in this world can never compare to the love, peace and true freedom that is found when we fully surrender to Jesus.

Instead of constantly striving to win approval through performance, I now stride in intentional steps in one direction. My entire purpose and top priority is to know him and make him known through my life.

With a transformed heart, I now run the race God has given me in his pace—
the pace of grace. I fully live from who I am in Christ, instead of from what I
do. I am loved, forgiven, restored, healthy, worthy, enough—and finally free.

> *And you will know the truth, and the truth will set you free.*
> John 8:32

---

*Amie attends Lifegate Church, where Les Beauchamp is Senior Pastor.
Her story was captured by Mike Hintz. For more information about Lifegate,
visit www.discoverlifegate.com*

11

The Sex Addict–
Integrity Is Within Reach

Edward Peters grabbed me in the Atrium one Sunday after church and burst out, "It's my one year anniversary!" I was just meeting him for the first time, so I said, "Congratulations! One year since what?"

"Since I was pulled out of the Missouri River after trying to kill myself," he said. "I was in a very dark place, but now my life is so different, so full of light."

Over the years, I had heard snapshots of the powerful work in Edward's life—and eventually we caught up for coffee, and I heard the whole story.

"When I was eight years old, my parents went through a harsh divorce. I wanted to discuss things with my mom, whom I have later understood to be controlling and shaming. She said, 'We're not going to talk about this.' And that is where I learned to stuff my feelings, which I did for the next forty plus years."

Edward continued, "A couple of years later, I was visiting my dad, who was living in a condemned house in Gainesville, Florida. I later found out he was a sex addict who had been arrested for lewd behavior. At ten years old, he introduced me to porn—a stack of *Playboy* magazines. It kept me occupied for hours, which made his life easier. For me, it was the start of an addiction.

"I continued to steal magazines through my early teen years and graduated to adult bookstores and movies by age 15. I began to crave the dopamine rush, the ability to escape reality for a few hours and especially the medication of the pain that I had stuffed deep inside.

"I married Caroline at age 21 in Ames, Iowa. I wanted to be faithful, but after our first child came, I started the affairs. Whether we lived in Ames or Greensboro, I always found the adult book store and escaped to watch my secret stash of videos. I was constantly on the hunt for my next rush, my next affair.

"But my addiction accelerated exponentially in 1995 when the Internet came of age and we got our first computer in the home. The Internet was like crack cocaine to the porn addict. It was faster, deeper, specialized and had infinite content. The first night we hooked up to the Internet, I maxed out our memory with porn downloads. In addition, the chat rooms made it far more efficient to hook up for affairs.

"I continued to steal magazines through my early teen years and graduated to adult bookstores and movies by age 15."

"I knew this was destructive, so I went through counseling, saw some specialists. I attended support meetings sponsored by Sex and Love Addicts (SLA). It is similar to an alcoholics' 12-step program, but it's designed for people whose addiction is sex. Caroline was patient with me through my addiction and affairs. She forgave me repeatedly, but Deborah was the last straw.

"Caroline and I had been married for 16 years, and she finally had enough. In 2001 our divorce was final. But I quickly married Deborah and started the pattern again.

"This whole time, there was nothing spiritual in my life. No Jesus, no church, no connection with God. In fact, I was offended when people talked to me about Jesus or their experience with church. I was 'just fine' on my own, thank you very much.

"The entire time I was married to Deborah, I was going to SLA meetings. I read books designed for sex addicts and wanted to stop, but my emotional pain was stuffed deep inside. I yearned for the approval I never got from my dad. I wanted to be accepted somewhere, anywhere. So I escaped on the computer. I had multiple affairs, seeking the dopamine rush that came from a risky and chaotic lifestyle."

In November 2015, Deborah had had enough. She told Edward, "If you do this one more time, I am leaving." He told me that he tried for about a month, but eventually slipped back into old patterns.

"I started crossing boundaries at work," he continued. "I always told myself before that I would never seek affection or sexual gratification with coworkers, but that changed. I started flirting, innuendo, sexting and sending inappropriate pictures.

"I was reported for sexual harassment at work for sending inappropriate pictures to a coworker. I knew my job was over. At the same time, Deborah filed for divorce.

"My marriage was ending. My job was ending. My credit card bills were stacked as high as a mountain. I was on anti-anxiety medication. Keeping all of my lies straight created so much havoc in my life that I was constantly on edge—as I tried to track my phone and my computer, hide my behaviors and remember the lies I told each person. I was exhausted from the charade and at the end of my rope.

"On April 12, 2016, I found out that the coworker I had sent photos to was sharing them around work to build a case against me. That was it for me. I knew I was sunk. So I went to a favorite spot on the Bluffs side of the Missouri River. I drank three quarters of a bottle of gin and took 150 anti-anxiety pills designed to make me sleep. I thought the combination would surely help me drown fast. I dove into the river and swam hard for the channel. I found that the water is excruciatingly cold in April. When I was just about to hit the channel, something hit me that said, 'I can't do this.' I desperately swam for shore, bleary from the alcohol and medication. I crawled my way out in the same spot I started. My cell phone was next to me. Cold and shivering, I called Deborah in desperation.

"Deborah called the authorities and the police and ambulance came. Next thing I knew, I was in a hospital.

"Three or four days in the Immanuel psychiatric ward can change your life. At that moment, my recovery truly started. Deborah kindly let me stay in the house until the divorce went through. I was on leave from work and experiencing intense anxiety. I went back to SLA two or three times a day. I was looking for something to do every day—even Sunday. One of my friends suggested Christ Community Church, where they also have a Christian-based sex-addiction group called Men of Integrity."

Edward reached out to CCC, and he immediately began attending both Men of Integrity and Sunday services.

"I snuck into the 'casual service' in the gym and sat in the back along the aisle. I hoped to remain invisible, but I was blitzed by the music, the words, the assurances. I bawled through the whole service. I felt the magnitude of the hole in my life in an instant. I had been looking for acceptance and approval through affairs and websites. My need was legitimate and massive, but I kept trying to find my approval in a sex addiction that always left me empty. What I realized in that moment is that I was actually yearning for God. I craved his acceptance, his approval.

"I had to reach up and trust God. My job was gone. My wife was gone. I went from a $65,000 annual salary to $11 per hour. I was $60,000 in debt and had to file for bankruptcy. I was going through withdrawal from my 43-year addiction. My body physically hurt from the withdrawal. My anxiety level was sky high because I was actually feeling my feelings and remembering my memories. I felt so guilty about my marriage failures that I gave her everything in the settlement except the debt."

The only thing that soothed Edward's soul was being in church.

"When I went to church or to Men of Integrity, when I spent time with God, something was different. I was actually feeling peace instead of escaping my negative emotions. I found if I could get peace from God for just five minutes, it rushed through my body like a physical flood.

"I cried during every service—often attending two in a row just to be in God's presence. And God helped me put my life back together.

"My long time friend, Bob, knew I was on disability and called me out of the blue to offer me a job the very next day. It was a small step at $11 an hour, but God was providing. In time, I moved from washing cars to selling cars. My income grew step by step.

"I tried dating websites, but nobody wanted to date me because I was now being honest about my past. I felt so lonely.

"I was just about to give up on eHarmony when Stacy came on. Despite my past, she agreed to meet me for coffee. We met at Panera, and I told her everything. I was shocked that she agreed to a second date.

"I was dating a woman who knew God, and that made our relationship totally different. My job situation continued to improve until I had a salaried job with benefits! My earning potential was restored.

"Today, I can stay sober because my life is full. That hole in my heart is filled by God. I have a purpose. I see my addictions for what they are. I can now walk beside other men who are on the same path and help them out. It takes years to work through the shame and guilt and replace them with a sense of love and forgiveness. Through all of this, God is restoring me and allowing me to coach others about God's restoration.

"Now I have hope. When I hit bottom, everything was gone. Now there is something to look forward to and a sense of fulfillment. Instead of hiding in my addiction, I hide in God. I go to him with all my problems, fears and insecurities.

"God is still peeling away the layers, getting at the core of my being. Case in point, I have cried more in the past three years than the last 50 combined. It has been key to my healing."

Edward has begun to embrace accountability to manage his addiction. He goes to CityCare Counseling and has put the accountability app, Covenant Eyes, on his phone.

"I have an amazing band of brothers at Men of Integrity," he said. And everywhere he goes, he snaps a photo with his phone and sends it to Stacy, so she knows where he is at all times.

"I recognize my emotions now," he said. "I know what fear feels like. I know what joy feels like. I know boredom, lonliness and significance. I can identify what is happening inside of me instead of just medicating my pain. When I am at church, I feel like my heart is expanding as I connect to the God of the Universe.

"I have forgiven my father and I don't need his approval anymore. But because I have God's approval, I am free.

"I am now a good husband and a good stepfather. I couldn't do that for years because I was trapped by my addiction. But now I am going to invest my life in things that matter and hopefully help a few more guys from the prison of porn to freedom in Jesus."

This story was captured by Mark Ashton, lead pastor of Christ Community Church. To contact Edward Peters, CCC, or the Men of Integrity, email info@cccomaha.org

12

The Couple in Crisis– Restoration Is Within Reach

She moved out three days after Christmas.

Kelly waited for Jake to leave for work, took their five-month-old son to daycare, and then started packing. First her closet. She stuffed the car "dangerously full" and dumped her clothes at her sister's house. Then she returned for another load—Baby Beckham's stuff. Then another load, and another.

Her obsessive-compulsive instincts demanded that she label each box, she says, but it was "organized chaos." She told me she shed a lot of tears that day.

All the while, she prayed he wouldn't come home. She didn't want to have another argument. She didn't want to listen to his point of view. He couldn't talk her out of it.

It was Friday. It was snowing. It was over.

Jake Foutch met Kelly O'Connor 18 months earlier, at Caddyshack, the Omaha bar where she worked. She gave him and his friends a ride home. And the next day, he found her on Facebook. (She jokingly calls it "stalking.") Their first date was at Kona Grill.

He was a 28-year-old who owned a landscaping business. He grew up in Valley, Nebraska and played baseball for three years at UNO—6-foot-5 left-handed pitchers are hard to find.

She was a 26-year-old a dental assistant who grew up in Ralston and earned her certification at Creighton.

That fall, they moved in together. They vacationed in Florida, and they conceived a baby. But by the time Beckham arrived in July 2012, Jake and Kelly were already having problems. The baby just made it harder.

"I thought I was doing the right thing at the time," Jake says. "Working harder, making money and having nice things. In all reality, I was just digging a deeper hole."

Small annoyances became huge disagreements. Growing up, Jake watched his parents experience rocky times. His dad found an escape in work. Now Jake was doing the same thing. When he and Kelly feuded, rather than addressing the problem, he walked out the door.

"It was the worst time of my life," she says. "I remember every month, every date, everything. It was awful."

Finally, she'd had enough. When Jake got home that Friday after Christmas, he didn't immediately notice. Not until he saw Kelly's empty closet. Not until he saw Beckham's empty room.

The first few days, he felt relief. No more fights. But soon the void hit him. "It was like dumping a bucket of cold ice water over your head." Kelly was still willing to talk, just not live with him. So he saw her and Beckham about once a week. That left him hours of time to think: What did I do? Who am I? Who do I want to be?

For the first time in his life, he opened a Bible on his own. He began to read scripture, especially the gospels. He watched sermons on video. He listened to Christian radio. He stumbled upon our church, Citylight. And about a month after Kelly moved out, he agreed to have coffee with me.

Jake told me he had noticed God in small ways: answered prayers, little doses of joy amid the daily grind. He was feeling more open to God. But that morning, for the first time, Jake emptied his guilt to another person. And then to God. Over several cups of coffee, he and I prayed and cried and prayed some more.

"That was my turning point. It was like the light bulb went on."

In February 2013, he invited Kelly to Citylight's first official service. She was already involved at Christ Community Church and wasn't really interested in changing churches. Or hanging out with Jake. They hadn't done anything publicly since they broke up. But she reluctantly agreed to go.

After that Sunday, they starting hanging out more. Breakfast. Dinner. Something had shifted.

Forgiving him was still hard. Just being with him was still awkward. But she'd been praying, too.

"My heart wanted to give up," Kelly says. "In every way I wanted to give up. The only reason I didn't is because I prayed. I'm like, God, if this is the person I'm supposed to be with, then don't let me give up."

By the time spring finally came, Kelly's heart began to thaw. They decided to try again, starting over. Only this time they were going to do it right. Separate homes. Sexual purity. More compassion. Better communication. They realized they had to go backwards in order to move forward. At the end of a typical evening at Jake's house, Kelly packed up Beckham and returned to her parent's house.

His friends thought they were crazy. Stupid, even. As his pastor, I tried to keep Jake focused on God and on healing his marriage. I encouraged him to rely on God, even when his friends didn't understand.

Even now, Kelly doesn't like to think about the year 2012. Pain resurfaces. Her stomach gets queasy. But she knows they're different people now. They both changed, grew. Jake insists that faith in Christ was the only thing that healed them. "There's no way we could've done this on our own."

He knows their wedding anniversary—Feb. 22, 2014. But he fumbles for the date of last summer's trip. "August..."

Kelly interjects "—Aug. 30."

Jake laughs. (He should probably know that.) He took the day off, and they drove to Kansas City. They stayed in the Plaza and spent the morning walking around. Jake kept his hand in his pocket, uncomfortably.

After lunch, they walked up to a fountain, and he stopped her. He tried to recite the words he'd memorized. He stuttered, stammered and mangled his speech.

"Honestly, it felt like I blacked out."

He remembers bawling before he pulled the ring box out of his pocket. And bawling after she said yes.

It was Friday. It was scorching. It was a new beginning.

Jake and Kelly's story was captured by Chris Hruska, Lead Pastor of Citylight Church. For information about the story, or about Citylight, , visit www.citylightomaha.org

13

The Drug Addict–
Joy Is Within Reach

Addiction is a powerful force, but God is more powerful than any addiction.

Daniel grew up in Minnesota, the son of an alcoholic dad, the brother of an addict as well. By the time he was 12, he was selling marijuana.

"I was selling it as a way to meet people," he recalls. "I love people, love connecting with people, and it seemed like an easy way to get to know people even more. I eventually fell into using drugs, after being around them for so long."

Daniel started with marijuana, then methamphetamines. From there, he experimented with mushrooms, heroin and cocaine. When he was about 19, he got arrested for the first time, for possession of drugs and driving under the influence of meth.

He was put in jail, but the judge let him out on probation. While on probation, he says, he was clean, but was still selling. "As soon as I got off probation," he said, "I went right back on drugs."

The next few years, Daniel continued to use and sell drugs. But a drug raid at the house he stayed at landed him in jail, and this time he wasn't given probation.

"It was October of 2012 that I went to Bible study in jail—and found Jesus," he says. Unfortunately, though he got saved, he was still caught in addiction and began using again.

Over the next several years, things did not improve. He fathered a daughter, who was taken in by the state because of his drug use. He believes now that being in foster care

"was the best thing that could have happened to her. I knew I needed to get out of where I was and start over."

While he knew his addiction was wrecking his life, he felt powerless over it.

"I didn't like where I was or what I was doing. I wanted to die, but I couldn't do it myself," he says. "So I started doing dumb stuff, like going places I knew I would get shot breaking down doors, things like that."

At age 32, he reached out to God in desperation, even as he continued to use drugs.

"On February 8, 2017, I started praying and asked God to save me. Two hours later, the Tricounty Taskforce knocked on my door." Surprised, Daniel says it was easy for the drug officers to know he was using drugs. "I blew marijuana in his face, and that gave them probable cause to get a warrant. They did a search of the house, and found marijuana, mushrooms, cocaine and meth residue."

Daniel went to jail in Wahoo, Nebraska.

After two months in jail, he went to drug court. From there, he was sent to treatment at the Stephen Center Hero Program. Getting into the Hero Program was his turning point.

"That really helped save my life. I met great people, started doing Bible studies and was challenged to start changing my attitude and stop faking my emotions. I started taking things more seriously—meeting with my sponsor, doing my steps, helping others who came through the doors and volunteering in the kitchen."

In the kitchen at the Stephen Center, Daniel met Chef Robert. "He became a huge mentor to me, giving me advice and growing me in ways I could never imagine. I actually started working for him in the kitchen and even continued working there for awhile after finishing the program."

The Hero Program allows participants to work at their own pace. It can take anywhere from five months to two years. Daniel worked hard and graduated in five months and two days.

Today, he is two years clean and sober and works as an assistant grocery manager. "I love my life," he says.

"When I'm asked how I got to where I am today, the only answer I have is that God's grace was on my life, and from the moment I asked for help, God put things in front of me to help me succeed," Daniel says. He sees all of it, even getting arrested, as part of God's plan to rescue him from addiction.

"Everything from the jail time to drug court to the Hero Program was put in front of me so that I could succeed. I could not have a better life, and I wouldn't change my past because now I am who I am today."

Daniel, who is now 34, helps others by serving as a sponsor. "I'm able to help others who are going through what I've gone through. I get to share what helped me and what I did in hopes that they would be able to follow the same steps into sobriety."

> *"When I'm asked how I got to where I am today, the only answer that I have is that God's grace was on my life... Everything from the jail time, to drug court, to the Hero Program was put in front of me so that I could succeed."*

Daniel lives in a Hope House through Mission Church. This is a transitional living program, where he lives with other guys who are also coming out of jail, treatment, addiction, etc.

"Through this program I am able to make new friends and work towards getting completely back on my feet myself! From being connected at Mission I've been able to gain incredible mentors as well. I currently meet with one of my mentors a few times a week at 5:00 a.m. to have prayer at the church. This has been an incredible time for me to continue growing in what God has for me in this season.

"Today I am an incredibly positive person. Since recovery, everything has been a step forward. I went from misery to joy!"

Daniel's story was captured by Amy Goepfert, Youth Leader at Mission Church, where Myron Pierce is Senior Pastor. For more information about his story or the church, visit www.thisismission.org

14

The Broken Marriage–
Forgiveness Is Within Reach

My counseling appointment with Charlie was short and to the point. I told him to call his wife and tell her to come home to work on their marriage. I told him to own his part of the problem, to admit his mistakes. Charlie called Felicia and said, "Pastor Hooker told me to call you and tell you to come home. I hate you and don't want to, but he told me to call." Even though Charlie didn't realize it, God was near to him even in that moment.

Felicia was in sunny California drinking wine and eating cheese when her phone rang with this less-than-attractive offer. Reluctantly, she agreed and booked a flight that very night.

Charlie and Felicia had seemed like a great couple when I did their pre-marriage counseling. Perhaps I missed some red flags or thought they'd be able to overcome any struggles they might have. They were both very good at hiding their imperfections.

Felicia grew up in a Christian family, went to church, taught Sunday school, obeyed the rules and asked for forgiveness after every sin. She knew how to play the role of the perfect Christian girl. Charlie also knew the Lord. He grew up at Bellevue Christian Center, the church I pastor. But he felt less "perfect" than Felicia, so he hid his sins. I recall, they were both very young but very "in love" and ready to start their life together.

They each began to make small compromises in their relationship with God and with each other. Charlie became addicted to pornography and hid it from Felicia. Felicia became so work-focused that she did not have time for God or Charlie.

Charlie had an opportunity to go on an unaccompanied military assignment to Korea. After his return, he said they could move back to Nebraska and start a family. This suggestion angered her! They were both very successful in California and life there was comfortable. She did not want to have any children and especially did not want to go back to Nebraska. Against her will, he decided to go anyway.

Feeling abandoned, Felicia acted out. Within a few weeks she was living the wild life. The perfect girl was no longer perfect. She was drinking and using drugs, and eventually she became pregnant.

Charlie was still in the practice of hiding his sin. He, too, was an adulterer, going to parties and getting drunk regularly. After hearing of Felicia's transgressions, he called all her family and friends and let them know who she really was, but he continued to keep his sins hidden.

Charlie filed for divorce, and Felicia signed the papers with tears in her eyes. She says she didn't even read the paperwork. Their marriage was now over. This "perfect girl" failed. But Charlie's sin was still hidden. He couldn't even see his own hypocrisy. They didn't realize God was within reach all during this time.

Charlie came to see me a few months after moving back to Omaha. I immediately suggested we meet regularly for counseling. I told him he had to own up to his mistakes, to confess to Felicia. He bravely called to tell her that he had judged her and that he was sorry. He confessed that he had made many mistakes as well, but he wanted to do things God's way, which meant divorce was not an option. But when he was willing to admit his part in the problems, the situation began to turn.

Our church prayer team also began to pray for their marriage. Additionally, their mothers and family members were praying fervently for them. Though Felicia and Charlie were unaware, these prayers would not go unheard. The Lord was active in their life even in the middle of their sin.

Despite her having a ticket in hand to return to Omaha, there was still the fact that Felicia did not want children, so she decided to have an abortion. When she approached the doctor's office, she locked eyes with a protestor urging her not to abort. She recalled how she had previously been one of these protestors. Just then, she was quickly draped by a black sheet over her head as she was ushered through the door. She wasn't sure if this was to protect her from the protestors or was her version of the Scarlet Letter.

She found herself in a room with three other women. One offered a pill to relax her. She took it, and the voices inside were quieted. She began to talk to the women surrounding her. One was having her sixth abortion. Oddly, Felicia began witnessing to her. Could it be that even in the abortion clinic God was near, within reach and active in the lives of people, even those who are in the process of having an abortion?

Now that Felicia was back in Omaha, I called them both to my office. I charged them to both draw closer to God and confess their sins, both to God and each other. The process proved life changing for them.

Eventually, Felicia gave up on her illusion of being perfect. She saw her need for the Lord and Savior and the importance of forgiveness. Charlie, who had a lifetime of hidden sin, now saw the importance of living transparently with his wife. This process was not easy. They spent months and months recounting their past transgressions and learning to forgive just as Christ forgave them. Admitting their own faults, rather than throwing blame at the other, changed everything. Forgiveness was now within reach, and it changed their lives and their marriage.

Today, Charlie and Felicia are raising five beautiful blessings from God: Judah, Micah, Noah, Jonah and Charlotte. Together, they are enjoying life as two parents who strive to reflect Jesus every day. They are not perfect, but they've learned God is perfect, and, as long as he is in the center of their relationship, they can work together to confess sin and forgive.

Felicia works in bookkeeping at Bellevue Christian Center. My wife, Melba, had the honor of participating in her hooding ceremony when she finished her masters degree at Grace University. Felicia supported Charlie as he graduated from UNMC as a physician. Charlie and Felicia are living proof that God is near, within reach and active in the lives of everyday, ordinary people.

Charlie and Felicia's story was captured by Walter Hooker, Senior Associate Pastor of Bellevue Christian Center. For more information about the story or this church, go go to www.bellevuechristian.com

15

The Husker Runningback– Transformation Is Within Reach

Listen, what do you do when you feel like you have everything you've worked your whole life for, but you still feel like something's missing?"

Matt Penland, chaplain of the University of Nebraska football team, sat across the table of the local breakfast joint and looked at the young man, wide awake even though it was 5:00 a.m. He'd heard this kind of question before, but he'd never met someone quite like Roy Helu, Jr.

Roy was an emerging star on the University of Nebraska football team. He had dominated at the high school level in Southern California, and his arrival on campus at UNL was highly anticipated. Coaches loved Roy's work ethic, players respected the way he could run through defenders, and fans across the state quickly noticed that Roy just had a different gear on the football field. While most college football players spent the majority of their freshman year on the practice squad, Roy was already playing and using his natural gifts to score touch touchdowns for the Huskers nearly every weekend.

But Roy didn't wake up before morning workouts and a full day of college classes to talk about football. Instead he was asking questions he had never asked before. Matt was impressed by his determination to find answers to the things that matter most in life.

At 18 years old, Roy was the big man on campus. His smile lit up the room, his frame displayed physical strength, and his play gained him public praise.

Still, Roy felt restless, unsatisfied, anxious and hungry for something greater than the world's applause.

That morning, Matt walked Roy through a few Bible passages from the book of Romans. Roy had been to church before, he'd heard about Jesus before, but that morning it was as if God was giving him fresh eyes, a new perspective. He began to see that what he was looking for would only be found in Jesus. Roy was used to being praised for what he could do for others, or for a team. But this morning, Roy moved towards Jesus as a man who had to receive new life, forgiveness and comfort from God.

"I came to Jesus as a guy who had made life all about me," he said. "My identity was football. My security was tied to how I performed for my coaches. I was obsessed with my external appearance. I didn't reject the notion of God, but I just didn't see my need for him.

"But God was gracious to give me everything I wanted, and then show me I had nothing apart from him. When I prayed that very humble, desperate prayer over breakfast, God met me and flooded my heart with a supernatural joy and peace. I knew, experientially, that Jesus was real. He did something in me in that moment—something I had spent my life trying to do for myself."

Roy wasn't trying to go from a bad kid to a good kid. He'd accomplished much and he had a bright future, even before that morning. But now, Roy had been changed on the inside. For the first time, Roy discovered that his identity wasn't tied to what he did on the football field, but to what Jesus Christ did for him on the cross 2,000 years ago. He discovered the joy of worshiping God, instead of working to be worshiped like a god. Roy found the freedom that comes by living empowered by the Holy Spirit and not living for himself and his ego. Everything was changing and soon Roy couldn't help but start telling others about what Jesus had done in his life. "I remember telling my teammates about my new faith in Jesus," he said. "Some of them were coming to faith in Jesus at the same time, and then I just stared sharing my story and the gospel with anyone who would listen. I got asked to speak at churches and campus events. I realized Jesus didn't just want to comfort me, but that he could use me."

Roy would go on to break records on the football field. His success in college athletics got the attention of the NFL, and after college Roy was drafted by the Washington Redskins. But Roy was not going to the NFL as just a guy who wanted to run the ball down the field for a team, he was going as a man who knew his identity was firmly rooted in Jesus. He had become a new man. He wanted his teammates, coaches and fans to see and know Jesus through him.

Roy would go on to lead team Bible studies for the Redskins, and later the Raiders. He saw family members and teammates come to faith in Jesus. Roy's story is a reminder that the human heart is restless apart from the One who created it and can calm it. Roy found joy not in making a name for himself but in making the name of Jesus great. His story is one of Jesus Christ giving supernatural peace to a man who couldn't find it anywhere else.

Today, Roy's story continues to impact others. He is a husband to Danielle, father of five and bold witness for Christ. Roy is a church planting resident at a local church and is asking Jesus to use him to plant a new church in Bennington, Nebraska.

"I believe Jesus has more for me and more for this city. I can't explain my story apart from Jesus, and my desire is to see many more come to know the same God who transformed my story. I'm excited about the next chapters to this story."

Roy's story was captured by Chris Hruska, Lead Pastor of Citylight Church. For information about Roy or about Citylight visit www.citylightomaha.org

16

The Inner City Survivor– A New Identity Is Within Reach

I should be dead.

Bullet holes riddled my dashboard. Blinding white light exploded around me. I have no explanation why I survived the shootout.

Except God.

Death shadows life where I'm from. The culture breeds a mentality of "me over you." Growing up with an incarcerated father and a struggling mother, I didn't have time to be a kid. The oldest of seven, I needed to provide for my siblings.

If we didn't have food, I stole to survive. If the water and electricity got shut off, I snuck under the cover of darkness to fill milk jugs with water from the neighbor's spigot. I always carried a gun for protection. Placed in foster care twice, constant tension riddled my life. Daily struggle defined my days.

I quit going to high school until I overheard a conversation between my mother and my little brother. When she tried to coax him to get out of bed, he asked why he had to go to school when I didn't. Talk about a gut check. I never considered myself a role model, but my siblings were watching me.

Going to night school, summer school and Saturday school wasn't fun, but I was determined to get my diploma for the sake of my siblings. After I graduated, I worked to help pay the bills. Unfortunately, I lacked direction, so I partied and got into trouble on the weekends.

A buddy invited me to a church retreat. When I got there and realized what the weekend was about, I tried to leave, but my car had a flat tire. I was stuck.

When I couldn't sleep, I wandered into the chapel, where two guys prayed for me.

As I left the retreat, one of the pastors handed me an envelope with $632 inside—$5 more than my mom needed to cover the bills so the lights could be turned on once again. This experience left me reeling. When I opened the envelope, I heard God speak. *You don't have to do everything by yourself.*

I decided to join the military so I could get custody of my younger brothers. I didn't want them to grow up with the same struggles I had. The military gave me a new perspective of the possibilities outside the inner city, but my frustration built. After two years without gaining custody, I was discharged and sent home.

Back home, I met my future wife and began working with Boys and Girls Club. Without me knowing, Chevelle signed me up to coach a third and fourth grade team through ABIDE, an inner-city nonprofit connected with Bridge Church.

I went to the coaches' meeting, and it didn't take long for me to realize this was more than just a coaching gig. These people had something I was missing: Jesus.

I wasn't sure how to get him, though. I remember listening to a podcast and hearing: "Show me your friends, and I'll show you your future."

In my search for identity, that resonated with me. I realized that continuing to hang out all the time with the boys in the 'hood would do nothing for my future. I didn't want to completely disconnect because I wanted to be a positive influence on my family and friends. However, I needed to be more intentional about setting boundaries so I wouldn't get caught up in criminal activity.

Working at Boys and Girls Club helped recalibrate my life, but I needed the right people around me to do life. I needed to surround myself with guys like Josh, Rob, Teddy and Ron at ABIDE and Bridge Church. Guys who invited me to attend a weekly Bible study at 6:00 a.m. and a discipleship class where I learned more about my life's purpose.

God spared my life the night of the shootout. Now he wanted to spare me from an eternity spent without him. In a men's group, I felt the Holy Spirit tell me to "be an example" and get baptized. Within the next month, I surrendered to God and got baptized as an outward symbol of the inner change. God was important before, but I wanted to make him central in my life.

That decision changed everything. No longer a victim, I became a victor in Christ. I had a whole new identity.

When I mentioned my love of videography, Pastor Rob Johnson gave me a chance to become an intern for ABIDE. Not long after, I partnered with two other young black entrepreneurs like me in a marketing business, with the goal of sharing the power of positive stories from our community. With my biracial heritage of Native American and African American roots, I want to be a communicator of cultures.

I want to impact the next generation. Through storytelling, using videography, blogging and social media, I want to be a positive voice. What we speak to kids is critical. Our voice becomes their inner voice.

My wife and I continue to help coach basketball through the youth program at ABIDE. We are expecting our first child, and I want to model a healthy marriage and family to the kids we impact, including my 11-year-old brother, who plays on the summer team.

My story is the story of countless kids in the inner city. Kids who long for love and direction. And somebody willing to impact a life.

Eddie is a member of Bridge Church where Josh Dotzler is the lead pastor. For more information about his story or Bridge Church, visit: https://www.bridgeomaha.org/

17

The Strip Club Bouncer– Provision Is Within Reach

It seemed like any other Sunday until Will came up and asked me to pray with him. When I saw this muscle-bound, tattooed man, my first thought was, "I don't want to make this guy mad."

"I think God wants me to quit my job and do something else with my life." His countenance looked like something between agony and fear. With a timid smile, Will went on to explain that he was a bouncer at a local strip club, and he had recently sustained on-the-job injuries that made him appear less intimidating and caused him to question his longevity in his profession. This may sound like a clear Sunday School situation. It's easy, right? He should quit his job, and God would probably bless him for his sacrifice of giving up an immoral life to pursue something less sinful. However, there is always more to the story if we are willing to slow down and listen instead of jumping to the end. Thankfully, this was one of the Sundays I got it right.

"What does your wife think?" I asked. What was left of his smile faded and concern etched his brow.

"You see, that's the problem. My wife is one of the dancers, and she doesn't want me to leave. I don't know what to do. What do you think?" His eyes brimmed with tears.

When I was pursuing life in the ministry as a young Bible college student, I did not expect I would someday deal with this type of situation. I thought people would want to know what the Bible says about marriage, friendship, giving or communion. Certainly, I didn't expect to be asked about strip club career options. I paused, asked the Lord for wisdom, and looked Will right in the eye. "What do you think God is asking you to do?"

"I think he wants me to quit, but I don't feel like Audrey will be safe if I am not there to protect her," he thoughtfully responded.

> *"Will, do you* really *think God cannot protect Audrey better than you? ...Maybe God is asking you to trust Him, and He will do something miraculous."*

"Will, do you *really* think God cannot protect Audrey better than you can?" I asked. "Look at your arm. You could not even prevent the injury you suffered. Maybe God is asking you to trust him, and he will do something miraculous." As the words left my mouth, I felt a sense of *where did that come from*. Truth be told, he was ashamed to bring this up to any other pastor, but my own sordid story made Will think I would seek to understand and not judge him. He was right. I did want to understand him without judging him or his wife.

I didn't know how God was leading Will; however, I got the sense that confronting Audrey about being a stripper and telling them both they should leave this work environment was not what God had in mind. I trusted him to speak to Audrey in his own timing, and I just focused on Will. Two weeks later, Will came up to me a second time.

"I did it! I quit my job!" Will's voice held hints of both relief and terror. "I just know that God is doing something in my family, Pastor. When I told Audrey that I made the decision, she was worried, but she trusted me." As happy as I was to hear Will's news, part of me was hoping there would have been a change for Audrey as well. But I know being in that industry can be like wearing golden handcuffs, and making a job transition can seem impossible financially. I was surprised, though, when Will continued. "That's not the only thing, Pastor. Audrey has also quit. We know it is going to be real hard, but if God is leading us, then he will take care of us." He had tears in his eyes.

I was so proud of them both for trusting God in this dynamic way. "We are here to walk this journey with you." I couldn't mask my astonishment.

In the months that followed, I saw the church truly become the gathering I think Jesus desired in the first place. Many people supported this couple, even though most of them didn't even know the full story. They gave money, prayers and referrals to new job possibilities. Even with all the support, this family struggled with the adjustment to a lower income. However, just like life, new rhythms formed.

Audrey discovered more time at home with the kids was beneficial to her heart. Will began working with children at Boys Town. He has found meaning and longevity in the work he does. Is the transition over? No. Is life perfect and easy? Not at all. Jesus never promised us an easy life. However, he did promise that he would be with us to the end. Somewhere in the middle of all of life's messy changes and transitions, two people are figuring out that God is more capable than they thought he was. They are discovering he is their provider and they don't need to be perfect. Like countless others pursuing the Lord, Will came to me in the middle of life's mess. I have a friend named Will who trusts God, and that is enough.

Will's story was captured by Mike Hintz of Lifegate Church, where Les Beauchamp is the Senior Pastor. For more information about the story or Lifegate, visit www.discoverlifegate.com

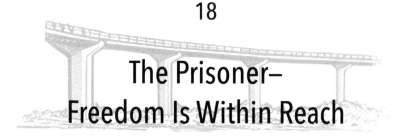

18

The Prisoner–
Freedom Is Within Reach

I grew up in the inner city, in a single-parent home. My life was full of chaos, dysfunction. Both of my parents were on crack cocaine. My mom was in and out of prostitution. Consequently, I started off in a life of crime and really felt drawn to the drug life, drawn to gangs. By the time I was 15, I dropped out of high school. By 16, I was facing my first prison sentence of 100 years.

Sitting in the Douglas County Youth Center, I heard a dude named Bobby come in; he was a chaplain. He regularly visited the center to tell us about Jesus. But it seemed like the reality of this Jesus and the reality of where I was living were too far apart. I call it the great gap. So I didn't give in to that Jesus thing because I didn't think it would work. I was too far gone.

Well, the judge sentenced me to only two to three years. So 14 months later, I was out on probation and back out on the street. Back out in the same neighborhood. Back out with the same friends. Five months later, I was back in jail facing 200 years. Nothing had changed.

At one o'clock in the morning, March 21, 2002, I got on the phone, right there in that little bullpen—a six by eight cell—and I called my grandma. By that time I was just weeping. "Grandma, I did it again." As I hung up the phone, I knew I was in a bad situation emotionally, so I fell to my knees. I looked up and spread out my arms and just prayed this really big prayer. "God, I'm destroying my life. But if you change me, I'll serve you for the rest of my life."

I can't explain it, but I felt something different inside of my heart. It was almost like I felt a love I never, ever felt before. And so as the judge gave me a 14- to 30-year sentence without parole, I was flabbergasted. I didn't know what to do with myself. I thought, what happened? I thought God was going to rescue me. So I walked out of the courtroom with this big, what I call a football number, and I heard this whisper in my heart. *Myron, I still have a plan for you. It's not over. Doesn't matter what you've done, I love you.*

> *"God I'm destroying my life. But if you change me I'll serve you for the rest of my life."*

It wasn't easy, but I kept my heart focused on the grace of God. I woke up every day and prayed. I went to work and did the things that I had to do. In prison, I was able to work on my education. Crazy as it sounds, a mere seven months later, I received a letter from the State of Nebraska that said: "Myron, we've changed the law. We're now opening up the door for you to get out in 2008."

And seven years later, by the grace of God, I got out of prison. And as I exited prison, I felt like God was saying, "I want you to be a part of providing hope. I want you to share your story about how God offers grace."

I ended up attending Grace University (they let me in by the grace of God). I ended up meeting my wife, who introduced me to a man named Ron Dotzler who started an organization called ABIDE, a ministry focused on revitalizing the inner city of Omaha, Nebraska, one neighborhood at a time.

Two weeks after we met, he extended the right hand of fellowship. "Myron, I'd love for you to come on staff." I didn't know that three months later we'd be starting a church right in the same neighborhood where I grew up as a gang banger.

This grace stuff, this forgiveness stuff, it's really free. I look over my life and all the people I've run with and all that's happened. I know I should be dead—or at least still in prison. But God loves me. And he's forgiven me. And he's shown me that his grace is enough. It's a free gift.

Myron Pierce is the senior pastor of Mission Church. Learn more about his story and the church at www.thisismission.org

19

The Skeptic–
Truth Is Within Reach

Tim Anstead is smart. Not just smarter-than-average.

Tim is Mensa-smart. He is six-sigma blackbelt smart. He can renovate your house, build your website or organize your event. He is he-could-win-Jeopardy smart.

Gretchen, his wife, is sweet. Texas sweet. French-silk pie sweet. Jesus-loving sweet.

If Gretchen wanted to go to her mega-church for her faith, Tim was smart enough to let her go and be supportive. But he wasn't going to buy into what he considered religious nonsense. Because faith is the opposite of objectivity, right? Faith is what you need when you don't do science, when you don't love evidence. Faith is for the naive.

This arrangement was working just fine until Tim and Gretchen moved to Candlewood Court in Algonquin, Illinois. As soon as they signed the contract, they heard about a Christmas party two houses up the hill.

This was all innocent enough, until they found out that a guy who worked at Gretchen's megachurch lived in that Christmas-party house. And he not only worked for a church, he was in the… evangelism ministry. Gretchen was elated, but Tim tagged along reluctantly.

As an intellectual agnostic, Tim worried that he would feel like fresh meat in the lion's cage at the zoo. He was so relieved to find that this was a non-religious party. Good food, tons of laughter, the reindeer poop game and Tim's favorite—the Christmas Trivia competition. Which he smoked.

No harm done. And those kids were so cute. Caleb, Caysie and Josiah were hyperactive animals who stole every neighbor's heart. Tim found himself visiting his neighbors from time to time—mostly to see those adorable kids. And actually liking it. He found that whenever they stopped to pray, two-year-old Josiah also had his eyes open and they could make silent inside jokes while everyone else talked to their God.

These were not the first Christians Gretchen had introduced to Tim. Tim loved to use his research skills to locate the hardest Bible-stumping questions possible to make believers squirm. And he had never met one who could stand up to his lines of reasoning.

One night, he brought his skills to the home of Mr. Evangelism staff—which, if you haven't guessed by now, is me. At about 10:00 p.m. one night, Tim said, "I know you're off the clock, but I was wondering if you wouldn't mind answering a few questions from the Bible—just from Genesis 1-11 that I was reading the other day." (Tim knew these passages are tough territory for a Christian to defend, so he went right for the jugular.)

Of course, off the clock or not, this is the kind of moment that makes my heart soar! So we jumped in. Tim asked questions about the age of the earth, the days of creation, the means of creation, the literal nature of Adam and Eve, the ages of ancient people, the literal nature of the flood and the Nephilim! I was blown away. But what impressed him was not the fact that I knew all of the answers (I didn't). He appreciated that I said, "I don't know," when I didn't know. He loved that I would give a range of options to answer certain questions. I'd say things like, "there are actually three views Christians hold on that issue; all are legitimate, and I tend toward option B."

We talked and laughed and fact-checked until 2:00 a.m. There were about three times when I had to say, "I don't know, but I'll do some research and get back with you." It gave me an excuse to get together again to restart the conversation at a more sane time of day.

A few months later, I launched a discussion group for spiritual skeptics/seekers, and Tim was the first guy I asked to join. About eight of us got together every week. It was scheduled for an hour and fifteen minutes, but the sessions usually ran three hours. You could count on Tim to do his homework and raise questions. He loved engaging in deep discussion with other intellectual, philosophical people. And he loved that it was a spiritual discussion, but Christians were the minority. We both stayed in the group for five years.

Every week, three hours a week. And yes, while I blazed the path spiritually, Tim renovated my house with me and built a website for my Bible Study guides.

Over the years we covered every subject imaginable:

- If God is good, why is there so much evil?
- Is Hell for real?
- What about people who have never heard of Jesus?
- How can you trust the Bible if it was written by flawed humans?
- Hasn't the Bible changed over the years?
- What about Jesus' outrageous claims to be God?
- Is the resurrection more like Greek mythology or Roman history?

Every week brought serious research and serious debate. Every week was filled with laughs. About 30 people came and went from the group, but Tim and I stayed from beginning to end. In fact, I began to ask him to help me with the "skeptics' perspective" when I trained my leaders. He even accompanied me on a mission trip to the ghettos of Costa Rica.

But faith was always an obstacle for him. After all the research and all the facts were gathered, he knew he actually had to trust God more than his own intellect. He had to let God have control—and this was his biggest obstacle.

After five years, God called me to move from Algonquin, Illinois, to Omaha, Nebraska, to lead a great church. The hardest thing about the whole deal was leaving my friend Tim. I told him about the new calling on my life, and we talked about how I hear from God. He was happy for me, but we were both pretty sad to part ways.

A couple of days later, Tim pulled up in front of my house in his big black pickup truck. He asked, "Does God speak to non-Christians?"

"Sure," I said. "In the Bible you have guys like Cornelius and Nebuchadnezzar. In fact I think pretty much everyone hears the whispers of God before they are a Christian. The game-changer is whether we will listen."

"Why do you ask?" I said with a grin.

He said, "I think God wants me to go to Nebraska, restart my business and hang out at your church. But I am not sure I believe in Jesus yet."

Tim and I met for breakfast at our favorite greasy spoon to unpack his calling. Through tears (mostly mine), he prayed to God with faith for the first time. We had a party at my house to celebrate. Caleb gave him a high five. Caysie performed a celebration dance. And Josiah still peeked at Mr. Tim while we prayed.

Tim moved to Nebraska and started his business. He later went on staff at Christ Community Church. He is the smartest church operations director in America and is chairman of the board for Rejuvenating Women. He and his wife, Gretchen, have adopted two girls.

Tim Anstead's story was captured by Mark Ashton, senior pastor of Christ Community Church. Learn more about Christ Community at www.cccomaha.org

20

The Drug Dealer–
A Healthy Marriage Is Within Reach

Tashiara Wilson dreamed of opening a house for abused women. She and her husband Tyrece had heard about our church, Bridge, and our Better Together Campus. They'd also heard I was the person to talk to about them.

During our great conversation, I told them about Bridge and invited them to come check it out. They began to attend Bridge regularly. As I got to know Tashiara, I came to appreciate her heart for women who had experienced the same type of pain and abuse she'd suffered. She wanted to start a ministry to those women. But it became apparent that she and Ty still needed to be ministered to—before they could minister to others. They were both wounded by their past, and they had a lot of healing to do in their marriage.

Both Tyrece and Tashiara had gone to church as children, but they never really thought God was within their reach.

"My grandmother sang in the church choir, so I had a sense of God's existence, but I never thought God wanted anything to do with me," Tyrece said. "My parents' addictions brought only chaos and dysfunction to my early years. Reckless living and selling cocaine as a young adult led me to drug abuse and homelessness."

He had big dreams of going to college and playing in the NBA. But, eventually, he gave up on that ambition. He began dealing drugs and ended up in prison.

Tashiara had grown up in church, but says she didn't understand what a relationship with Jesus meant. The fact that her mom took her to church growing up but lived a different lifestyle outside of church made Tashiara not only skeptical but rebellious.

"Hungry to fill the void left by an absent father, I partied and slept with anyone who took an interest in me," she said. "Pregnant at 19 and in a violent relationship with yet another man, I cried out to God."

As a single mom, she had no interest in getting married or even dating. But, she says, "I felt God promise me that I would be married within the year. I was skeptical to say the least."

She met Ty at a concert in Kansas City soon after that conversation with God, and she says, "I knew he was God's promise to me. However, Ty had been in and out of jail, including two years in the penitentiary for robbery. My family and friends thought I was a fool for marrying him."

She was going to church, and she believed Ty was the man God promised to her.

"Because everything I knew about marriage I gleaned from watching TV, I had no clue how to be married. So I tried to make Ty into something I wanted. Our marriage unraveled before we even began. If I really wanted help, I needed to get serious with Jesus. I was hopeless and headed for divorce."

At one point Ty had lost another job, and they were on the verge of being homeless. They came to me for assistance. Finances were a challenge, but their deeper relational problems were an even greater obstacle. I asked if they were willing to do "whatever it takes" to turn their lives around. They said yes. We moved them and their two children into a room in one of the dorms on campus. A family of four living in a dormitory isn't ideal, but it was a step in the right direction.

Ty began to spend time serving on our campus, and through a partnership, he was able to get a good paying job. For over a year Ty worked for Thrasher, a basement and concrete repair company, and began to grow in his role as a father and husband. We began to see incredible progress in his life.

But even though they were making progress, things weren't perfect. One day at Bridge, Tashiara told me Ty had been out all night and wasn't doing well. I sent her and the kids to our house with my wife, and I went to visit Ty. He was shocked to see me show up uninvited. I asked what he was doing. We made little progress through our conversation, so I invited him to go on a run. I knew he had been out all night and likely was not in the mood for a workout, but I also knew he wasn't being honest about what was going on.

I decided I would push him to his limits, both physically and relationally. On that four-mile run, I gave Tyrece what he calls "the hard truth." I challenged him to get real. I told him it's easy to blame the other person, but he needed to work on himself. He needed to change his family by making changes within himself.

The day ended with Ty, Tashiara, Jen and me in our backyard, chatting. Jen and I helped them reconcile and see a new vision for what life could be like.

"Josh's brutal honesty helped me come to my senses," Tyrece recalls. "If I didn't do something, I would lose everything. Desperation brought me to God. Without help, I would lose my marriage, my kids, everything."

> *"I had no clue how to be married, other than the fairy tale marriages I saw on TV, so I tried to make Ty into something I wanted. Our marriage unraveled before we even began."*

Coming to Bridge, he realized something critical. "If I wanted real change, I needed to make a commitment to Jesus. I'd already thrown in the towel with my dreams to go to college and play for the NBA, but this time I had the desire to push through the challenges. I prayed, 'Help me, Jesus. I'm all in.'"

I could see that Ty and Tashiara had a heart for ministry, and I always hoped they would join ABIDE, the nonprofit connected with Bridge Church. But I knew Ty needed to continue to be faithful with the job he had before we could take the next step. Over a year after working his new job and consistently making progress, I asked Tyrece and Tashiara to come on staff with ABIDE. They became lighthouse leaders in one of the targeted neighborhoods in the inner city.

"I never saw myself as a leader impacting others for Christ, especially since I'd been dealing drugs for over 10 years," Tyrece said. "But God was moving in my life and giving me boldness I'd never experienced. As lighthouse leaders, our task was to intentionally build relationships. As I was learning, being a Christian was a lifestyle. Being discipled and discipling others could only happen in relationship."

When Tashiara and Tyrece began loving their neighbors, many of whom were refugees from Thailand who spoke little to no English, they were astonished to see how their neighborhood began to change.

"People began picking up trash and hanging outside, even planting flowers together. Neighborhood grill-outs and basketball games brought a new sense of community. The language of love crossed all cultural and language barriers," Tyrece says. "Every day I made it a point to hang outside with the goal of being intentional and available. One of the fifth-grade neighbor boys even confided in me, 'You don't know what it means to me for you to be outside every day. It makes a difference in all our lives.'"

Tashiara noticed the change in Ty. He was seeking God and had found a sense of purpose, which gave her a new respect for him. "I stopped trying to sabotage his leadership of our family and began to trust his decisions," she said. "If Ty was God's promise to me, I needed to stop arguing with my husband. Our kids noticed the changes. Because they'd lived the craziness, they now soaked up the new love. Our three-year-old daughter told people she wanted to marry someone just like Daddy. Even our 10-year-old son commented about the love between us."

Tyrece is growing in wisdom and learning how to respond to God's promptings. He admits he sometimes is uncertain, "but I'm learning to pray and listen for God to respond," he says.

He told me about a situation where God spoke and helped him really love his neighbors, even in the midst of their pain. "Recently, one of our neighbors asked for help. Her dad, an alcoholic, beat her mother. Clueless about how to respond, Tashiara and I prayed about the situation for several days. Not long after, I noticed my neighbor (the dad) sitting outside on the porch. I heard

God nudge me to respond with love. So that's what I did. I ran over and gave my neighbor a big, long hug. His eyes watered as I looked him in the eye and said, 'God gave you your wife to love her—not to beat her.' Since that exchange, my neighbor hugs me every time I see him, and I'm beginning to see changes in both his family dynamics and the care he is taking with his yard."

Being intentional about living out a lifestyle of discipleship together has strengthened Ty and Tashiara's marriage. "When I see my wife minister to our neighbors, I'm blown away with her value as a person and the incredible gifts God has given to her," Ty says. "Before, I took Tashiara for granted, but now I am quick to compliment her."

Ty and Tashiara discovered that a healthy marriage was within reach, and they marveled how God used their improved marriage to impact others. "Only God could have breathed life into our broken marriage," Ty says. "When we wanted to quit, he surrounded us with a family at church who wouldn't let us give up. When we were hopeless, God changed our hearts and restored hope. What an amazing God we serve."

This story was captured by Josh Dotzler, lead pastor of Bridge Church. For more information about the story or this church, go to www.bridgeomaha.org

21

The Desperate Mother–
Rescue Is Within Reach

My wife and I sat at our dining room table, listening to Linda as she poured out a story of horrific pain, terrible circumstances, utter darkness. And yet, also a ray of hope, of light. Rescue was within reach.

Twenty-seven years ago, Linda told us, she had tried to leave what had become an emotionally- and physically-abusive relationship. She told her husband she wanted out. He responded by taking their newborn daughter in his arms and—in an unthinkable act of horror—squeezed the life from her body while Linda watched in agony. Helpless. Terrified. Devastated. Words cannot describe the darkness that invaded her soul in those moments.

That darkness became an inescapable prison of fear and hopelessness for her and her children. Convinced that she too would die if she attempted to escape her husband, Linda pleaded to God for help.

And help came.

Help came in the middle of the night when, in response to the desperate pleas of her extended family, the Mexican Federales arrived on Linda's doorstep to rescue her and her children and whisk them away to freedom.

Then again, freedom isn't always what it appears to be.

Linda was free from the imminent danger of her husband's threats and fury. Yet, the burden of fear, bitterness and self-hatred was so excruciating and suffocating, drugs became her only means of momentarily relieving the pain.

Unknowingly, she exchanged one prison for another.

And who can blame her? Who can fathom the depths of despair that would drive a young mother to look to drugs for things like pleasure, rest and the ability to feel happiness again?

As my wife and I listened to Linda share her story, I tried to take in all the details without letting my mouth stand agape.

The most remarkable detail about her story isn't losing her daughter or being rescued by the Mexican authorities or even living in the throes of addiction for two decades. The most remarkable detail about Linda's story is that she is alive to tell it.

Martin Luther King Jr. once said, *"Darkness cannot drive out darkness; only light can do that. Hate cannot drive out hate; only love can do that."*

For years, Linda attempted to drive from her mind and heart the darkness that had engulfed her life from the time she was a young child.

But it didn't work, because darkness can't drive out darkness. Only light can drive out darkness.

Listen to Jesus' words in the Gospel of John.

> *"I have come as a light to shine in this dark world, so that all who put their trust in me will no longer remain in the dark."* John 12:46

Jesus Christ came to illuminate the darkness of abuse, rage, hatred, bitterness, addiction and the innocent loss of life. He came to set us free from the tragic consequences of our own choices to live our lives apart from him. And he came to heal us from the words and actions of those who have caused such pain and heartache in our lives.

Recently, Linda discovered that there is a God who knows her by name, created her for a purpose and sent his own Son to die in her place. To forgive her completely and offer her a brand-new beginning filled with the prospects of a joy, peace and hope.

When Linda beheld the beauty of Jesus Christ for the very first time, she invited him to rescue her.

And Jesus did rescue Linda.

And he continues to rescue her to this day.

When Linda gave me permission to share her story, I asked her if there was a verse of Scripture that has played a significant role in her journey of faith.

She pointed to Jesus' words in Matthew 19:26...

> *"Humanly speaking it (salvation) is impossible. But with God everything is possible."*

When you, or someone you love, stands in the middle of a dark night, remember that Jesus came to illuminate the darkness and show us the way back into the arms of our Heavenly Father. He is the One who makes all things possible.

Linda's real name was changed for her protection. Her story was captured by Jed Mullenix, Lead Pastor of First Christian Church. For more information about the story or this church, go to www.firstchristiancb.org

22

The Abused Wife–
Light Is Within Reach

Shayla met her husband when they were teenagers, at Iowa Assembly of God district youth camp. He was a pastor's kid and a bad boy flirt, but he chose Shayla. From the beginning, Shayla thought they were going to do ministry together. She knew his true rebellious personality, but she believed that, if he had enough support, then their life together could be really good. After they got married, they lived in Waterloo, Iowa, and had two boys together.

The couple struggled from the very beginning of their marriage. They struggled financially. Marc rarely went to church, which caused conflict. He had a hard time keeping a job, and he started drinking. They lost their house. They decided to start over and move to Omaha. Of course, their issues came along with them, and he chose to cope by drinking excessively.

The more he drank, the more violent he became. As many abuse victims do, Shayla excused his behavior. When he said he didn't mean it or he was sorry, she believed him. She rationalized, "At least he's not hurting the kids," but some of the violence and pain transferred to the kids when they tried to protect her and got in his way. This pattern brought a lot of sleepless nights, and Shayla frequently got up the next morning and pretended like nothing was wrong.

For a long time, she didn't say anything to anyone. She hid it from her family, until her sister moved from Minnesota into the apartment building next to Shayla's. When things got rough, Shayla would take the boys and hang out in her sister's apartment. But she didn't want her sister to know how bad things really were, so they sometimes stayed overnight in hotel rooms. Shayla took the kids to the movies just so she could get some sleep.

Shayla didn't believe she and the kids were safe at home. A few times, Marc's sister tried to intervene. She knew things were bad and wanted to protect them from her brother. One time she took the kids and tried to convince Shayla to let them stay in Iowa. The reality of being alone with him at home terrified her, so she brought the kids back home, a decision she now deeply regrets.

Shayla ended up working a lot of overtime to support the family, but her husband believed she was having an affair. Because Marc so strongly believed Shayla was cheating on him, he argued that he could cheat on her. Marc denied Shayla's suspicions, but when she finally had proof, he never apologized. He wanted her to share him with other women. She just wanted him to pick her again. She just desired for her family to be together. She held onto the dream that they were going to be in ministry together one day.

The violence escalated to strangulation and death threats. One time, he even cut himself. When he refused to go to the hospital, he made a bloody scene on the apartment balcony. Eventually his choices led to seven months in jail. Shayla didn't visit him, but she wrote to him. She told him about the things of God, trying to get him to change. She didn't even really know how she felt about him or the marriage because her feelings were all over the place. She didn't feel like she needed her husband to survive, but she fell into a depression. She waffled between blaming herself for his circumstances and knowing that he needed to take responsibility for his own actions.

When he got out of jail, they started meeting with me. We talked about everything— their past, the abuse, the alcoholism, all of it. Everything came out in the light. Until then, it had just been festering in the darkness, growing into this ugly monster. However, confrontation and boundaries didn't seem to change her husband. He wasn't interested in God, or in changing.

During this time, I could see Shayla felt alone and forgotten by God. She told me she was holding onto a proclamation she made at youth camp. She believed that if Jesus had not done anything more for her than die on the cross, he would be enough. It's what she stood on when God seemed far away.

She wanted things to be different, and she knew she had to do something different, so she joined different support groups, such as Al-Anon and DivorceCare. Al-Anon, a group for family members of people who have alcoholism, taught her that she must take care of herself before she can take care of others. She learned that she could not change her husband. The only thing she could change is how she reacts to different situations. She went through DivorceCare twice because she was so mad about her situation and the possibility of divorce. Eventually she came to a place where she knew her marriage wasn't working anymore. She chose to believe that God had more for her life than suffering through these circumstances. She told me she felt like she was on a merry-go-round. Things would seem better, but then they weren't—over and over and over again. She finally wanted out.

She filed for divorce without telling her husband. She just let him get served with the papers. He was frustrated that she didn't tell him, but she just wanted to be done. She told me it was one of the hardest things she's ever had to do. To her, divorce is such an ugly word. She never wanted to get divorced in her life. Even checking the box when filling out a form is hard. She felt so alone.

Through it all, God showed her that he knows her by name. He showed his love for her by blessing her with a safe, beautiful home where she could raise her kids. God gave her strong friends who encourage her. God blessed her with a new job that is healthier for her. I knew God wanted to use her in great ways.

I had hope for their marriage, but I knew it was dependent on him wanting to pursue a relationship with God. He, however, wanted his own way and alcohol more than he wanted his wife and kids. Since the divorce, I've seen her blossom. Before, darkness and shadows held her back from using the gifts God has given her. I watched God grow Shayla into a beautiful young lady who has so much to offer. Now, she is excited and open to new possibilities. She knows God still has plans for her life. He can and wants to use her to do great things.

Shayla's story was captured by Walter Hooker, Senior Associate Pastor of Bellevue Christian Center. For more information about the story or this church, go to www.bellevuechristian.com

23

The Sad Girl–
Freedom from Shame Is Within Reach

The first time I observed Ally, I saw a girl trying not to be noticed. She would sit in the back, avoid eye contact with me and the other pastors, then scurry out the sanctuary doors right at dismissal to avoid having to talk with anyone.

I tried to overcome her reticence with kindness. Each time she came to church, I'd loudly greet her in my signature booming voice, "Ms. Ally, how are you doing this week?" I'd give her a big old side hug, and that's how it went every Sunday morning. I was unaware of what God was doing in her life, but nonetheless he was working.

Only later would I learn of the rescue mission God was carrying out on behalf of this incredible, gifted daughter of his.

Ally's childhood was not particularly difficult or traumatic. Her family was supportive and caring. She had many fond childhood memories to cherish. However, in her heart, Ally daily wrestled with sadness. She seemed to be easily wounded by even minor difficulties. So she floated between social groups, trying to find her place, but never feeling like she belonged.

The morning of April 26, Ally found herself in a psychiatric ward. No family and no friends in sight, only strangers and a chilling loneliness and fear. The day before, Ally had told her friends she was going to kill herself. Her friends, alarmed, relayed the news to her school's administration, who took her threats seriously. Now, as she sat on her hospital bed, the humiliation of being escorted to a police car during school dismissal rushed back to her mind. She wondered if life would ever be the same. If her friends would see her differently from now on. A resolute thought crossed her mind... *God's not real.*

In her mind, a real God would keep this from happening—or at the very least get her out of this hopeless mess.

When she was released from the psych ward, things got much worse. Ally stopped caring and started numbing her pain by drinking, smoking and doing drugs. Her closed-off, I-don't-care attitude didn't win her many friends. But there was one girl in her school Ally desperately wanted to be friends with. She was one of the most talented people Ally knew, but every time Ally would invite her to parties or hang outs, the response was always "no thanks."

Instead, this young lady invited Ally to church, where she spent a lot of her time. Still adamant that religion was a waste of time and God wasn't worth the effort, Ally always declined her invites to Bible study or church.

But one day, Ally finally caved. After all, maybe going to church would change the way others saw her after her trip to the psych ward. She asked her mom to take her, and they headed to the church.

As they drove, doubts assailed her heart. What a mess she was, she thought. She became painfully aware of the scars she carried, both physical and emotional, from self-harm and past hurts. The shame and embarrassment of her journey thus far sat on her shoulders like a weight as she approached the church door. Her steps grew heavier and more reluctant. Anxiety tore at her heart as she reached to open the door. And then came the moment which would change her life forever.

As she pulled open the door, a sweet breeze swept gently over her face. And Ally, unaware that God could speak to her, felt a whisper inside her head. "I'm not embarrassed by you."

This voice let loose a torrent of tears, releasing years of pent-up shame, dark thoughts and deep pain. Ally wept as she entered the building. Late for service, she came in to see her friend on the worship team singing the refrain, "This is the year all of your tears will be dried."

In that moment, Ally knew God was the rescuer she had been wanting, needing and waiting for. She had no idea how, but she knew God had brought her to this church. In that moment, he had intervened in her story. That reassurance from God made her feel safe and loved. She found herself wanting to know the God who had whispered that sweet assurance.

The change in Ally's life was marked and astounding. Ally left drinking, drugs and self-harm behind and never looked back. In retrospect, Ally can see God's orchestration of her coming to him, like the threads in a giant web.

She would remember a school assembly she'd attended in middle school, where she had met church leaders who would later be instrumental in her discipleship. She remembered past friendships with Christians, encounters with Christian music.

Looking back, she could see all the small pieces in God's intricate plan to rescue her. Even when she rejected God, he was wooing her to himself.

Every year on the anniversary of her stay in the psych ward, April 26-28, something significant occurs on one of those three days. For 15 straight years, God has made sure there is a pointed reminder of the significance of her story. Whether it's an opportunity to share at a youth conference, her speech at a D.A.R.E. conference or a private reminder between her and Jesus, he is faithful.

Ally doesn't avoid me in the foyer any longer. I've had the privilege of watching her heart blossom as she has discovered deeper purpose, identity and healing in God than she ever thought possible. God rescued her from despair. Hers is a story of hope, healing and redemption, and God has only just begun!

Ally's story was captured by Walter Hooker, Senior Associate Pastor of Bellevue Christian Center. For more information about the story or this church, go to www.bellevuechristian.com

24

The High School Student–
A Loving Family Is Within Reach

My family doesn't believe in God. I live at home at my grandmother's house, along with my mother and my twin sister. Sometimes I stay with my God-mom as well. At home it can be difficult because my family doesn't know God yet, although I hope to be a part of changing that!

Every Thursday during the school year I would walk my cousins up to this church, where they attended Good News Club, an after school club for elementary school students. I am a sophomore in high school, so I was too old to attend.

I really wanted to hear what was happening though, so I would wait in the back for them each week. While I waited for my cousins, I met two women who helped run the club. Esther and Cheryl became incredible mentors to me. I started to listen to the lessons they taught the kids at the club. I heard about all different kinds of Bible characters. I had never really heard of them before. Miss Esther was super nice to me; she even invited me to come to church on Sundays as well. I wasn't sure about this, and it took me a while to be able to go.

During the summer, there was no Good News Club for my cousins, so I wasn't able to attend. One day though, I decided to go to church on a Sunday morning. I live two houses down from the church so it is an easy walk to get myself there! When I was there, I saw Miss Esther and Miss Cheryl. Little did I know they had been praying for me continually since Bible Club. I really enjoyed attending church, and I continued to go.

One day, Pastor Myron offered an opportunity for people to give their lives to Jesus. I went up front to do so because I felt like I was supposed to that day. Miss Esther came to stand with me, and our pastor spoke over me. He told me I was going to be a leader, and that Esther was supposed to be my mentor. Miss Esther told him how I had been at Kids Club every week, and that they had been praying for me ever since. A few Sundays later, I was baptized, and I am able to live out my new life in Christ.

Now that I have been attending Mission regularly and said yes to Jesus, my life has changed! I attend youth group, and I also help lead our New Beginners group, where I help youth and adults who have just said yes to Jesus. In our last class there was someone extremely special to me. My twin sister. La'Shawn started coming to youth group and then church with me. Now we both get to help Miss Esther with different Bible Clubs in schools in North Omaha. We get to impact students of the younger generation. My twin sister was baptized in March, and now we are both living our lives for Jesus.

This summer I'll go to camp to learn how to teach kids about Jesus all summer! Then, I'll get to go with a team to do week-long kids camps all summer—and even get paid some to do so! I attend CRU at my school, where I get to interact with others who believe in God. I've even brought some of the kids to youth group with me. I meet with Miss Esther who mentors me, and Miss Cheryl is an incredible mentor as well. They always find fun things for us to do! Esther and I do a Bible Study, and I am able to continue learning more and more about the Bible and all that happens in it. I attend 6:00 a.m. prayer every single Sunday. I'm learning to be more confident in leading and praying out loud, as well as sharing what I want to hear from God, or what I need from him in this season. I also serve on our creative team and help to run our live stream every week!

Without God in my life, I would just be another high school student trying to survive, without anything to back me up. My life before Christ was pretty lonely. I wasn't very positive and I was doing everything on my own.

But now, I am able to pursue my relationship with Jesus every single day. I have Christ-centered friends who pray for me and rally around me. I have leaders and mentors who help me get places I need to go or are available to listen to me and encourage me. I have incredible friends from church, who welcome me into their homes often. I love being able to grow in Christ with them, as well as be able to support them when they have something they are going through. My support system is greater than it ever has been, and I am thankful for the family of believers I found when I entered in the family of Christ!

My desire and my prayer is that my family would follow in the steps of my sister and come to know Christ as well. The feeling of standing next to my sister as she was being baptized was something I never want to forget. I pray that God would bring the rest of my family, too.

Ka'Shawn's story was captured by Amy Goepfert, Youth Leader at Mission Church, where Myron Pierce is Senior Pastor. For more information about his story or the church, visit www.bellevuechristian.com

25

The Alcoholic's Daughter–
Faith Is Within Reach

Anna's earliest memories of family were ones of tragedy and confusion. She shared several memories with me.

When she was a small child, two homes she lived in were destroyed by fire. During the second fire, her mother had tried to save the family cat, and then found herself trapped on the second floor. She had to jump and broke her leg. This resulted in Anna's older sister taking over to care for her siblings. The family was forced to move to a hotel.

Anna also knew her mom loved to drink what she called "soda." She recalled this conversation with her sister shortly after one of the fires...

> "My oldest sister, Isabel, mumbled as she stood over the hotel room's tiny kitchen stove. The wooden spoon clanked against the metal pan as she pounded the ground turkey to crumbly bits. I listened to her muttering to herself, 'Maybe if she didn't drink so much... alcoholic parent... can't even function.'
>
> Those words, I thought. What is alcohol? What does Mom drink that's so bad?
>
> 'What is that?' I asked. 'Those words you're saying?'
>
> Isabel's back went rigid. She slowly turned from the stove. 'What words?'"

This led to a frank conversation with Isabel about their parents' alcohol addictions, and the revelation that the fires may have been the result of her mother's drinking. Mom's "sodas" were unhealthy. Isabel told her how their mother loved them, but she had a real problem. At the end of this very frank conversation, Isabel asked, "Are you okay, Anna? I didn't hurt your feelings, did I?"

Anna remembers telling her sister, "I'm never touching Mom's sodas again."

Isabel told her, "You may not understand the severity of it now, but someday you'll see."

Young Anna replied, "I understand plenty. She's choosing the drink over us."

Isabel and Anna continued to have these painfully honest talks. Isabel did her best to guide her sisters away from their mother's destructive behavior and jaded view of family. These conversations were a real confidence builder for Anna.

However, as Anna got older, she started to hang out with friends who loved to party. She frequently lied to her parents about where she was going and what she was doing.

"Though I hung out with a rowdy crew, I had the most common sense out of the group," she recalls. "I drank liquor and smoked with my buddies, but I refused to party every weekend. No way will I grow up and develop the same issues my parents faced. Booze will never control me."

By the tenth grade, Anna was abusing alcohol herself. She was headed down the same path as her parents.

When Anna turned 16, her mother began to practice Wicca. She had many conversations with her mother about spiritual things. When Anna was a kid, her grandmother had taken her to church where she had heard about Jesus. Her mother's Wicca beliefs only served to confuse Anna and make her question what she had learned at church.

"I concluded she was right. The Bible made no sense whatsoever," she says. "Too many biblical characters shared similar life stories to mythological gods. Plus, the Bible appeared to be full of contradictions and physically impossible tales."

After high school, Anne moved to Las Vegas for college. She experienced several bad relationships with guys and decided to focus all her time and energy on work and school. Then came Eli. He totally "messed up" her plans.

"Eli turned out to be anything but a roadblock," she remembers. "He encouraged me to concentrate on my studies and accomplish every goal I set. He told me that one of his goals was to return to church. He told me he believed in God but couldn't seem to find the time for God in his life. He asked about my take on God. I told him that I believed in God and Jesus, but not the Bible. Eli thought that was an odd combination, and suggested that we go to church together someday. I knew the only reason I'd go was to further strengthen my Bible-bashing beliefs."

The two did not go to church, but they did continue their relationship, and after college, they got married. They moved to Omaha and started a family. Two years after the move, Eli's father was diagnosed with stage four cancer. His dad was a true believer in Jesus. His attitude toward life and death was baffling to Anna.

Anna remembers a visit with Eli's father, where he sat down with his family and said, "I know the family is worried about me. But I'm not concerned at all. If God plans for me to enter heaven sooner than any of us anticipated, then I'm for it. Of course, I hope there is more work for me to do on his earth, but I trust God."

She remembers thinking, Is he nuts? How can he have such blind trust in God?

Later, she cornered her husband as he put the baby down for a nap. "Your dad is either insane or the epitome of a faith," she said.

"My father trusts in God's plan," Eli told her.

Anna wasn't sure what to think. The faith, courage, peace and grace that Eli's father experienced through his sickness and even to his deathbed impacted both Eli and Anna.

Eli's dad left a present for him. Anna remembers Eli showing her a worn Bible, with a note inside from his father. It read: "I know you have your reservations and doubts about the truth of this book, but I want you to know God."

Eli told Anna he wanted to know Jesus the same way his dad knew him. "We have to find a church that will help me develop whatever Dad had," he told her.

Later Eli's friend Steven invited them to Flatland Church. During their first visit, Anna leaned over to Eli and whispered, "Dude, these people are so different. How can they be this nice? How are they so welcoming and open to total strangers? Don't you find that bizarre?"

He shushed her. "Stop it. Stop questioning everything and enjoy today."

"I shut my mouth and let my husband enjoy the service."

The sermon that morning was about Jesus and his interaction with the woman at the well.

Despite Anna's determination to keep her guard up, she was moved by the story. She thought, "Oh, man. This lady kind of sounds like me. She didn't belong, but he pursued her anyway." As Anna sat there, she remembers, "Tears gathered and fell as a rush of guilt washed over me. Prickly sensations skittered over my body. What in the world? Why am I tearing up like this? Head bowed and eyes clenched shut, I tried to conceal my sniffles with fake coughs. I knew why I was crying. It was these people and this guy's message. I walked through these church doors with such bad intentions. I'm a total outsider. A disbeliever. I'm a woman on a mission to disprove something these people love. I'm sure they saw the judgment and condescension written all over my face. Yet they talked to me. Welcomed me. Why?"

Why indeed! Because, as the church, we are called to love God and love people.

That Sunday was a turning point for Anna and Eli. They were won over by the love of God, shown to them by loving people.

What a joy it's been to see Anna and Eli grow in their faith, become leaders in the church and love many others into the "Kingdom of God."

This story was captured by Kelvin Nygren of Flatland Church, where Bart Wilkins is the lead pastor. For more information about the story or this church, go to www.flatlandhurch.com

26

The Baseball Parents– Transforming Power Is Within Reach

I n my experience, more lives are changed while watching kids' sporting events than are on most typical Sunday mornings.

This might not be the most popular thing for a pastor to say, especially one who values job security as much as the next person. But it's undeniably true, as I was reminded while sitting in the dust-covered, boiling-hot grandstands of a rural baseball field during the summer of 2017.

When I met Jeremy and Kelli, they would say they were about as far from God as they'd ever been, but the truth is that God was closer to them than ever before.

I got to know Jeremy and Kelli as we watched our kids play baseball. Soon enough, I learned their story. The emotional and financial pressures of Jeremy's unexpected unemployment, combined with an underlying frustration around the trajectory of their lives, had led to a growing unrest in their home and marriage. While Kelli thought about reaching out for hope in her local church, Jeremy wasn't buying it.

Jeremy and Kelli would say they attended my church, because their kids were very involved in student ministries at FCC. But Jeremy had only been a handful of times in the ten years they'd lived in Omaha. Kelli was more spiritually open, but even she attended only a handful of times each year. They'd typically drop off the kids, and we'd see them only at baseball games.

In his experience, the church wouldn't or couldn't offer anything he was looking for. Not adventure, or security, or peace, or joy or purpose. Nothing.

Yet, it was when Jeremy was unwilling to look for God that God came looking for him!

I believe that God gives us children for a hundred different reasons, not the least of which is so that he can supernaturally open doors for surprising friendships to be formed between us, their parents, and their peers' parents. I probably sat next to Jeremy at more than 50 games, and we had at least that many conversations. There was never one moment that I could point to as a crucial conversation, but we just became friends. Their kids became friends with our kids, and we went out to meals at state tournaments together. We were simply baseball parents together.

Before my son joined the same team as Jeremy and Kelli's son, I would've never imagined connecting with Jeremy on a heart-level, much less calling him a friend. He is a burly, bearded, beatnik-loving hipster who kills deer, deep-sea fishes, bakes chocolate and lemon-blueberry tarts and sips exotic coffees from Yeti mugs. He will undoubtedly be a candidate for the next series of *The Most Interesting Man in the World* commercials.

On the other hand, I've never been accused of burliness, ever! I'd rather sit on a beach than crouch in a deer stand. I didn't know that tarts were makeable. And when I've attempted to grow a beard in the recent past, I've been accused of looking icky and creepy. It's a strong description, but the right description.

Still, God somehow stirred a friendship between us that has taught me the life-changing potential of what can happen when we prayerfully look for ways to love the ordinary people who cross our path during the ordinary moments of our everyday lives.

God even works on miserably hot days in rural Iowa.

That summer, I was able to watch in real-time as Jesus wooed Jeremy and Kelli's hearts back to Him. I sensed a softening, a new curiosity. Then one Sunday, Jeremy and Kelli showed up at church. The next week, they were there again. Six weeks later, Jeremy placed his faith in Jesus, and Kelli recommitted her life to Jesus.

I watched their closed minds open, their hardened hearts soften and their heavy souls set free from the crushing burden of navigating things like disappointment, discouragement and fear without the knowledge of a God who loved them enough to pursue them, even on their worst day.

Jeremy would say that going through unemployment, after having been successful in business and respected in the community, actually changed him for the better. God used that difficult season to draw both Jeremy and Kelli to himself.

I had the privilege of baptizing Jeremy and Kelli later that summer, before our family left for our summer vacation in Massachusetts and Maine.

Two summers later, their family joined us on our vacation in Maine.

Recently, Jeremy shared this with me about the transforming power of Jesus' kindness and mercy in their lives.

"God has moved in every facet of our lives," he said. "He's brought our family closer together. We're serving Him. And we've made radical changes in our lifestyle in answering the call to his Kingdom. Where God has worked the most incredible miracle is the people he has put into our lives. His church has wrapped its arms around us, and saying yes to Jesus has changed everything."

Isn't that beautiful? A family who used to run away from Jesus now runs after Him!

What's equally as beautiful is that before they said yes to Jesus, Jesus said yes to them. He pursued them before they were even looking. He died for them before they were even searching. And he called them by name before they were even listening.

Jeremy and Kelli's story was captured by Jed Mullenix, Lead Pastor of First Christian Church. Learn more about the story or the church at www.firstchristiancb.org.

27

The Desperate Mom–
Clean and Sober Is Within Reach

Addiction defined my early life.

Every day was a land mine of chaos and insanity. My parents were both addicts. My earliest memory is walking by my sobbing aunts at my dad's funeral. I was three, too young to understand that my dad lost control of his vehicle because he'd been drinking. The oncoming motorcycle he hit crashed through his windshield. My dad died 24 hours later. His death caused my mother to spiral into schizophrenia. She partied to cope.

Darkness filled our home. Abuse and neglect were the norm. Hiding my mother's lies was mandatory. Anger and fear kept me chained. I didn't know any other emotion. I was angry with my mom and angry with God, but too afraid to change the only life I knew. My mother's partying and bouncing from man to man, along with the physical abuse, the instability and mental illness left deep scars, traumatizing me.

Desperate, I sought emancipation and moved in with my best friend's family at age 14. Running away only added to my problems. I turned to alcohol to forget the pain, becoming a full-blown alcoholic by my 18th birthday.

Pregnant at 22, I promised to give my son a life full of joy and happiness, but I had no clue what happiness even looked like. Clueless about how to release the pent-up anger and fear, I continued to party to mask my pain.

Getting introduced to meth only compounded my problems. Meth numbed me. Not being able to feel was the best feeling I'd ever had.

Numbness came with a price. When I gave birth to my first child, love swelled within me. Despite the longing of my heart, my unstable world of an addict hurt the one person I loved the most in the entire world—my son. My addictions exposed him to countless men, domestic violence, cheating, lying and bouncing from place to place.

Somehow, I had become my mother.

When God gave me another chance at motherhood, I swore I would change my ways. But when Child Protective Services showed up at the hospital the following day to place my infant daughter in foster care, pain like I'd never known knifed my heart. Leaving the hospital empty-handed killed me. I lost track of time. Day after day, I lay on the bathroom floor unable to function. For the first time in my life, I cried out to God—whoever God even was.

When I cried out, a surge of strength came over me. This God I didn't even know empowered me to enroll myself in outpatient treatment. Six months later, I got my daughter back. To this day, I know she is truly one of God's miracles. My daughter—a gift—is beautiful, smart, perfectly healthy and chosen.

Thinking my addiction was only to meth, I drank throughout treatment and continued in the months that followed. Not long after I got my daughter back, I had another daughter. Though I loved my children, unresolved pain left me empty. I'd built a great sober support system through my time in treatment, but as soon as I stopped surrounding myself with positive people, I fell back harder and faster into my old addictions and bad relationships.

Consumed by my addictions, I lost all control of my life, and in October 2009, Child Protective Services took all three of my beautiful children. Because I was using meth again, I'd not only hurt myself but contaminated our home enough to expose my children to the drug. Hearing in court that my kids tested positive for meth sent me over the edge. My life was over. I amounted to nothing. I would never be able to mother my children. I was done fighting. My kids were finally safe. Ending my life would be the best thing I could do.

How can I put my pain into words? The bond between a mother and child is so intense, the devastation of losing them was more than I could handle. To cope, I took pills. Lots of pills. Strung out and convinced my dealer was going to kill me, I jumped out of a moving vehicle on the interstate.

Miraculously, I survived, breaking only a few teeth and shredding some skin. Disowned by my family, only one aunt, a Christian, visited me at the hospital. When she told me how much Jesus loved me, I knew there was something better than what I had known. Completely ready to surrender, I asked my aunt how to get Jesus into my heart. She prayed with me, and hope exploded within me. I was ready to fight for sobriety and fight for my kids. With God's help, I walked into treatment in January of 2010.

Getting substance abuse and mental health treatment at the Stephen Center HERO inpatient program helped me understand the underlying issues behind my addictions. I began to ask God to help me change my perception and practice new thought patterns. Suddenly I gained a sense of responsibility I'd never known. I learned that if I wanted to get better, I had to forgive those who hurt me. I had to learn to forgive myself for the things I had done—not only to my children, but everyone I encountered.

I had no idea how to have a relationship with God, so my aunt invited me to a weekly Bible study hosted in my grandmother's backyard. A former addict, my grandmother met Jesus in prison at age 69. Growing together brought much healing. Today, seven of my grandmother's children attend the same Bible study. We're all praying my mom will surrender soon.

Accepting Jesus' love and forgiveness changed my attitude and my outlook. God continues to work miracles in my life, and the gifts keep coming. When I stay in constant contact with God and pray for the knowledge of his will for me, peace floods me. I have a boldness for who I am in him. I no longer live in fear. I have healthy relationships today. Relationships where love, honesty, patience, acceptance and kindness shine.

My life is no longer defined by my past. Rather, my life today is full of happiness and opportunity. As I look back on the past 10 years, I see Jesus in all things.

- Jesus gave me courage to surrender to self and beg for help.
- Jesus helped me get sober after being addicted for 20 years.
- Jesus walked with me from bus stop to bus stop looking for employment.
- Jesus battled beside me through a 22-month juvenile court case to fight for my children.
- Jesus reunited our family and taught me how to be a mother.
- Jesus showed me how to be fully present for my kids. We even travel together—a blessing I didn't experience growing up.
- Jesus walks with me hand in hand as I set goals and achieve them.
- Jesus walked across the stage with me to graduate from college—something I never thought possible.
- Jesus gave me the chance to meet the motorcycle driver my dad hit. Embracing one another brought healing for each of us.
- Jesus changed the trajectory of my family.

Today, I am the director of the same shelter where I broke my addictions. Jesus helps me walk alongside other women who are fighting to get sober. Many times, I find myself sitting on the front steps leading one of our clients in a prayer of surrender to Jesus. I've found my purpose. Jesus has blessed me with life-lifting empathy. God *chose* me to share hope and encourage others to surrender. He daily equips me beyond my own abilities.

I didn't know how to be a good mom, so my church family at Bridge came alongside me and helped me learn. They have poured so much love into me and my children, each of us is learning to love with a heart like Jesus. Because Jesus is so good, I have the family I never dreamed I could have. Weathering the storms together has made us stronger. Our home is full of love and light.

Addiction no longer defines my identity.

Beth is a member of Bridge Church where Josh Dotzler is the lead pastor. For more information about her story or Bridge Church, visit: https://www.bridgeomaha.org/

28

The Gang Leader– Victory Is Within Reach

Years ago, as part of a home mission spotlight, I heard Servando Perales speak of the Victory Boxing Club, a club he founded to help kids get off the streets and to experience God's love. He was a person with a deep passion for his work. When I sat down in the office of Victory Boxing to hear his story, I came to understand the roots of his passion.

Servando told me of his childhood and described a tragically broken home. His father was a hard worker, but he struggled with alcoholism and regularly abused Servando's mother. He remembers going with his mom and siblings to find his father and help bring him home from whatever bar he was drinking in.

At age nine, Servando and his brother found refuge at the Downtown Boxing Club in Omaha. Kenny Wingo, a boxing coach there, took Servando under his wing. Beyond coaching, Kenny became a father figure to him. Boxing lent purpose to his life. By the time Servando turned twelve, his father had abandoned the family, leaving him, his mother and six other children.

In his book, *The Cry of a Warrior,* Servando writes of his success as a youth boxer. He became a national champion at the age of nine and was a Golden Gloves contender. Yet, even with this success, he succumbed to the allure of drugs and was kicked out of South High School in the tenth grade. Servando described to me how by the age of eighteen he and his clique, the Latino Boxers, had progressed from using drugs to selling them to employing others in their enterprise. He became an established dealer and gang leader in control of the South Omaha drug trade.

Servando became addicted to meth, and getting high became the focus of his life. He was becoming progressively more violent and hurting others. Like his father had abused his mother, he became abusive toward the woman who would later become his wife. Eventually, Servando was arrested on federal gun charges and sentenced to eighteen months in federal prison.

After his indictment, Servando was initially sent to a holding facility in Leavenworth, Kansas, where he met Frankie. He knew of Frankie from his criminal past, but something had changed in Frankie's life. Frankie had encountered God. He told Servando, "God loves you." Servando wasn't interested. He simply wanted to do his time, get back on the street and once again exert his influence over the South Omaha drug trade.

Servando was eventually transferred to a federal prison in Waseca, Minnesota, to serve the remainder of his sentence. One day Michelle, Servando's future wife, called him to tell him that Frankie was coming to Waseca. Frankie now played the guitar, and in prison chapel services he would sing songs he had written. He invited Servando to chapel. At chapel, Servando experienced the kindness of volunteers who came to the prison to serve the inmates. He was moved by two older women who brought cookies. Their love and acceptance surprised him. They told him, "We're praying for you. God wants to use you." Servando told them, "You don't know what I have done." And yet, the love of God expressed through the volunteers' lives impacted him. He began to reflect on his life, the people he had hurt, the grief he had caused his mother, how like his father abused his mother, he had abused Michelle. He realized he shouldn't even be alive. He cried out to God from his cell, "If you are real, come into my heart and change me... save my life!" Servando felt God respond, "Yes, Servando, yes!"

Servando knew he needed to call home and tell Michelle. Michelle had stayed with Servando all this time, and he realized her love for him. He wanted to do whatever he had to do for her and his young family. He told Michelle, "I've accepted Christ, and I am changed. I'm going to be a good husband and father!"

Michelle said, "You are kidding me." She went on to explain that the very night before he called, Michelle had gone to a friend's house with Servando's sister. This friend told them of Jesus' love, and they, too, had surrendered their lives to Christ. Servando and Michelle found a new foundation to build their lives upon.

Servando's life had taken a remarkable turn from imprisoned gang leader to Jesus follower. When he got out of prison, he and Michelle were married. He learned that two of his friends from the gang had also surrendered their lives to Jesus. He and his friends called their old gang together. Servando confessed to his former gang that he had used them, and he was sorry. He called them to surrender their gang vests, and they cut them apart. The gang was no more.

Servando also returned to the passion of his youth—boxing. He began to train, took off the 25 pounds he put on in prison and went pro. After amassing a 7-1 pro record, he went to Las Vegas where he fought on the undercard of the Evander Holyfield - Lennox Lewis fight. Sevando lost. After that loss, at twenty-seven years of age and struggling financially, Servando concluded that boxing was a young man's game, and it was time to move on. He said he felt the Lord say, "You are already a champion. I have another fight for you."

Servando returned to Omaha with a new dream to start a faith-based boxing club to reach the youth of South Omaha. One day in church the pastor asked, "Does anyone here have a dream?" Servando found himself on his feet testifying of his dream. Encouraged by the church, Servando began his club in his garage. He worked any job he could to support his family and support his dream. Eventually he found support in the community. His first major supporter was the same police officer who had arrested him on the gun charge which sent him to prison. That incident, a seeming setback, was what set him on the road to his very real encounter with God's love.

Servando's dream, Victory Boxing Club, now thrives in South Omaha at 30th and R Streets. Young men and women learn to box, find fellowship and community, attend Bible study and experience the love of God through Servando's dream becoming a reality.

Servando Perales—drug dealer, gang leader and federal prisoner—was never out of the reach of God's love. Now God relentlessly pursues the lives of young men in South Omaha through the life of a once-broken, South Omaha boy who has been transformed by God's indescribable love.

Servando's story was captured by Gary Hoyt, Lead Pastor of Bellevue Christian Center. For more information about the story or this church, go to to bellevuechristian.com.

29

The Wounded Couple—
Marital Restoration Is Within Reach

Dan and Pam met in a small town in Kansas when he was 23 and she was 19. They married and began a life together, but they struggled from the beginning. Many of their difficulties came from wounds they carried from childhood. But even when we are wounded, God is within reach and can bring healing.

When I met with Pam and Dan 20 years later, things were quite a mess. Dan was broken and needed healing from insecurities which had him in bondage. Pam was hurting because she was struggling to be perfect in her own strength and she couldn't control all that was going on in her world.

Because Pam moved a lot when she was younger, she had not ever developed long-standing relationships. She naively assumed the long-term commitment of marriage would just magically happen. She found it challenging to deal with disagreements. When they had children, she focused on being the best mom she could be, but in the process Dan was left to take care of his own needs.

Dan had suffered loss as a child. Two of his brothers had passed away—one as a newborn when Dan was two years old and the other of leukemia when both he and Dan were teenagers. As a teen, Dan had begun to use pornography to feel better about himself. Despite his intentions to stop, he continued that habit when he got married.

Dan and Pam, despite their own pain, thought they might be able to minister to others, so they took a class on Christian counseling. When the topic subject of sexual abuse came up, Pam nearly vomited. For Pam, the topic triggered something in her—she wasn't sure what. Later, when Pam found out Dan was using pornography, she was caught off guard. Her own pain collided with the shock of her Christian husband viewing pornography. She felt confused. But both of them stuffed their pain.

For 20 years, they were married but isolated. Neither knew how to get healthy emotionally or spiritually.

Dan felt at times like his only value was to be a "paycheck." He felt like they didn't need him, just his money. He felt so worthless he thought about trying to commit suicide. But he didn't want his daughters to have to deal with their dad taking his own life.

Pam was a strong person for everyone except herself. But she felt lonely because she had high expectations of Christians, and she would back away from anyone when she saw their imperfections. Everyone including her husband.

Dan tried many things to get control over his battle with porn. He counseled with me over the years, attended Every Man's Battle weekend and met with a Christian counselor. All the information was helpful, but the struggle was still there. God revealed to Dan that he succumbed to this sin because he felt isolated and was trying to fill the void in his heart. However, all this helped lead to a turning point.

Pam's frustration was so high she stopped sleeping in the same room with Dan. She continued to try to fix things by attending a small group called The Sexually Confident Wife. She attended Every Heart Restored weekend and learned boundaries in marriage. Yet things did not change.

Finally, Dan and Pam attended a Cleansing Stream retreat, and it proved to be a turning point for both of them.

At that retreat, Pam was reminded that despite Dan's mistakes, God still loved and cherished her husband. She also learned that God could heal their marriage. Initially, Pam was angry, but she realized she needed to forgive Danny. She finally stopped feeling sorry for herself.

Dan began to understand the truth that there is a spiritual battle for his heart, which started even when he was a child. He learned that no one person could meet his needs, but that God could meet all of his needs.

Through the journey God did not give up on Dan. God pursued him and led him. Pastors, counselors, leaders and friends encouraged him. Dan began declaring the truth of God's word and found new freedom in Christ.

Now Dan may feel lonely at times, but he no longer believes the lies of the enemy who says he's not important. He knows he is loved and valued. He now respects the differences in how he and his wife each see things and wants to hear Pam's thoughts.

Pam is now more merciful for those who struggle because she sees that she, too, is imperfect. She has learned to forgive and move forward. Pam is confident in hearing from the Lord. She feels like Dan respects her opinions and feels open to share more than she ever could before. They have more appreciation and understanding for one another. They now share deeper levels of intimacy emotionally, spiritually and even sexually, and they continue to grow together.

Dan will tell you that without forgiveness, transformation is not possible. Forgiveness becomes possible only in a relationship with God. He realized that when he dealt with the pain of the past, he could move forward into all that God had for him.

Dan and Pam were married, but they lived isolated and alone until they allowed God to heal each of them. Now they are truly serving the Lord together!

Dan and Pam's story was captured by Walter Hooker, Senior Assoc. Pastor of Bellevue Christian Center. For more information about the story or this church, go to bellevuechristian.com

30

The Teenage Single Mom— God's Family Is Within Reach

ngela grew up in Omaha in an Italian-American family that rarely went to church. When they did go, it felt to her like a punishment. She didn't understand what was being said and frankly, God did not seem relevant to her life that was filled with chaos and abandonment. Angela's dad went to prison where he eventually died, and her mom took to the streets using and selling drugs. When Angela's older brother died in a car accident when she was 14, her disinterest in God turned to anger and hatred. Her brother was her rock of safety and now he was gone. Angela planned his funeral and sold drugs to pay for it.

At 15, Angela had her first child. That same year, she was arrested on drug charges and was sentenced to a year in county jail. That's where she met Chaplain Eunice Arant, who loved her and told her about a God who loved her. There, those seeds were planted, but still being in rebel mode, Angela returned to the same situation where she had another baby and landed in jail for a second time. That's when Angela started to pray.

When she was released, life started to come together. Angela married, had another son and worked at a real job. When she left her abusive husband, lost her job and needed help, a friend told her about Citylight Church. There, she found a completely different community and desired to know this Jesus everyone seemed to know and love. She dedicated her son, Troy, to the Lord, got baptized and became a member. Angela has the gift of serving and joined just about every team imaginable, including driving the church van to the Open Door Mission to bring people to our worship gatherings on Sunday mornings. She began to experience healthy community, and in some ways she was thriving.

Under the surface, however, she was still running from her past and holding back areas of her life from Jesus. She thought she needed to figure things out on her own, and she ran right back to the life she was so familiar with. Her church family was heartbroken and discouraged as weeks turned to months, yet none of our efforts to reach out were welcomed. But God was not finished. He pursued Angela even when she was in prison.

When she was in another jail cell, she heard the song "Oceans." The song reminded her that Jesus was still there, pursuing her. Angela cried out to him and admitted her sin and rebellion. God opened her eyes to see him clearly. She felt him all around her and slept peacefully for the first time in a long time. She felt his assurance that he was giving her another chance.

By God's grace, Angela was released to the Lydia House New Life Recovery Program while awaiting sentencing. The Citylight van came on Sunday morning, and she jumped on. She knew the path she needed to take and was all in this time. She realized that when she was the van driver, she thought she was better than the people she was picking up, but now she was one of them. In that moment of humility, she was grateful for God's hand leading her out of the fire. Tearfully, she thanked the driver and walked in to worship with her church family.

Jesus told his disciples there is joy before the angels of God over one sinner who repents. When Angela humbly stepped off the church van and walked through Citylight's doors, Jesus showed us a picture of that kind of celebration. We rejoiced with her, squeezed her tight and reminded her that she is a child of God and he would never let her go. She embraced community in our church and reconnected with Eunice Arant and the recovery group she leads on Monday nights, New Community.

Surrounded by her biological family, church family, New Community family and Lydia House family, Angela faced the judge, expecting to be sentenced to 77 months in federal prison. Instead, God showed his abundant mercy. She was sentenced to just five years of probation. Angela knows God saved her from death, prison and ultimately an eternity without Him. She knows he saved her for a bigger purpose and lives each day growing in her relationship with him and others.

Angela's gift of serving landed her a job on our church facilities team where she blesses us with her work ethic and desire to make our space beautiful for the glory of God. And on Sunday mornings she joyfully serves on the van team once again sharing the truth that Jesus is there when we cry out to Him.

This story was captured by Sarah Buettenback, Serving Teams Director at Citylight Church, where Pastor Gavin Johnson is the Lead Pastor. For more information about the story or Citylight, visit www.citylightomaha.org.

31

The Lost One–
A New Direction Is Within Reach

Alan was about 13 when his older brother and a friend came home with some vodka and challenged him to chug it. Little did he know how that choice would change the trajectory of his life for many years.

He told me about that night. "It was midnight, but exhaustion evaporated as the alcohol made its way down my throat, scratching and burning. My brother and Josh smiled. They looked so proud—my brother most of all."

His brother's approval and attention inspired Alan to continue drinking. He went on to do eight shots and received more "positive" feedback from his brother. At the moment, he was proud of the fact that he had downed more shots than his brother did his first time!

That was followed by his introduction, that same night, to smoking marijuana. They both went outside with another friend and they spent the night getting high and listening to the Kottonmouth Kings rap about the joys of smoking weed. This was the start of his downward spiral into addiction and all that goes along with it.

He soon had a girlfriend who enjoyed getting high and drinking as much as he did. Soon, the girl was pregnant. She pressured him to tell his parents about the pregnancy, but he hesitated. Of course his parents did eventually find out, and he got the "lecture" from his mother. His response was to escape into drugs.

"As the pipe shop receded in the background, and we hit open country," he recalled, "I grabbed the plastic bag from my buddy, unwrapped the pipe, lit up and let my worries evaporate with the smoke."

Alan hadn't heard from his girlfriend for several days when he got a phone call from her wanting to talk about alternatives concerning her pregnancy. She was seriously considering abortion, which Alan was strongly against. They went their separate ways.

Later, he got a text from her saying she was on her way to the abortion clinic. He tried to text back, but his phone went dead. When he finally got the phone powered up, there was one text waiting: "I did it."

"It felt like a knife slit me open and hollowed out my insides," he says. He told himself not to think about it, to try to forget about it. "Trying to cauterize the wound, I drank myself to oblivion. We broke up after that, mostly becase we each reminded each other of our grave mistake. The day she got an abortion, our relationship was tossed in the trash along with the baby."

Failure continued to haunt Alan's life. His grandfather was very ill and had moved into Alan's parents' home. His mother asked him to look after his grandfather and give him his pain meds every hour. He agreed and set his phone to go off every hour, then fell asleep. He woke up the first hour and gave his grandfather the medicine. He went back to sleep but failed to wake up the second hour, and he was late giving him his pain med. When Alan woke up the next hour, his grandfather wasn't breathing.

"He wasn't supposed to die when I was watching him," Alan says. "He was supposed to die when we were all awake. Tears rolling down my face, I shuffled to my mom's room, softly shook her shoulder and told her, 'He's gone.' Crying, I went outside and smoked half a pack of cigarettes. That's not how I wanted him to die. Not on my watch. Full of grief and remorse, I hated that I'd failed everyone—again."

Alan continued his drinking. After drinking at a bar one night, he decided to try to drive home. He was drunk and got into an accident, and the police issued him a DUI. He was injured, angry and afraid of what his dad was going to do. With the weight of his guilt growing, he became despondent.

"I kept making the same mistakes over and over again," he says. "I didn't stop the killing of a baby. I had failed the expectations my parents had of me—hell, even the expectations of my parole officer. The conscience I had been smothering for years through intoxication was screaming at me. I'm tired of this shit."

Despondent, Alan picked up a rifle that was in his home. But it had no ammunition.

"So I grabbed a 12-gauge shotgun, found ammo and felt the weight of the cold, loaded gun in my hand. Whatever. I walked upstairs and left the DUI ticket in front of my parents' bedroom door, then walked downstairs and out the front door. I made it a few houses away before I realized I had forgotten my cigs. I placed the gun in the chilly, dewy grass, went back inside to grab my pack and returned to the gun. Its weight was nothing compared to the weight of the mistakes I'd made. I figured the silence it would bring would be much better than bearing this echoing burden, better than constantly running away from the pain—or so my drunken self whispered. The fluorescent lamps lit up the street I'd grown up on, making the wet grass glow and the concrete glitter. It was cold. It was quiet. I held the gun to my head. BANG!"

Alan did not succeed in killing himself, but he did manage to injure himself severely. Being stuck in the hospital for many weeks, he got clean and sober for the first time in a long time. Once he healed up, he started working for his father.

One Sunday he decided to show up at Flatland Church with his family. People welcomed him, and he was glad to be in a place where he felt loved.

Alan was listening to the song "Take Me as I Am" by Lecrae. The words focused on God's forgiveness and grace and spoke clearly to Alan's soul.

"I'd been going nowhere fast. I'd been given warning shot after warning shot—the abortion and multiple DUIs. Even after an actual shot to the head, I still didn't realize it. God was trying to get my attention, trying to call me to himself, saying 'only I can satisfy.'"

Alan was moved to tears. Echoing the lyrics he prayed, "God, I surrender my life to you. I have nothing to bring you except my sin-stained life and a record of wrongs. I cannot change on my own. I need you. Forgive me, Lord, for running away, for rejecting you. Lord, take me as I am."

I am glad to say that Alan's prayer was answered. He became actively involved in ministry and began sharing his story with others. He's recently married, clean and sober and a shining example of God's grace and transformative power. He had been going nowhere, but now he has found meaning and direction by letting God lead his life.

Alan is not his real name. This story was captured by Kelvin Nygren of Flatland Church, where Bart Wilkins is the lead pastor. For more information about the story or this church, go to www.flatlandchurch.com

32

The Engineer–
A Purposeful Life Is Within Reach

I am white, and my wife is black. I was born and raised in a rural town of 300 people in Iowa. My wife was raised in Washington, D.C., with over five million people.

We met in college, married, started a family and lived a comfortable Christian life in the suburbs. We attended church several times a week and read our Bibles, all the while amassing houses, cars, and other possessions in some vain attempt to "keep up with the Joneses." We have a large family: fourteen children. Our favorite Bible verse is "Be fruitful and multiply."

I didn't consider myself materialistic or absorbed in conformity, and yet my bank account and lifestyle proved otherwise. Somehow, though I was completely unaware, the American dream had swallowed me up.

Without realizing it, I'd built a cocoon of protection that insulated my family from a broken and dangerous world. I'd prepared my family for financial success so that nothing could penetrate the safety net surrounding us.

And yet, no matter how hard I tried, satisfaction eluded me. Outside of my family, friends and career, I longed for a greater sense of purpose in my life. While I'd heard people talk about knowing God's calling for their lives, I'd never experienced that reality.

Something was missing.

In this season of growing emptiness, God piqued my attention through a Christian tract I saw in a public building. The booklet instructed a new

Christian on how to live: "Now that you've given your life to Jesus, read the Bible, pray, go to church and do good."

Do good struck a chord in me. The stark contrast between this *nice* version of Christianity and the *radical* Christianity of the Bible stopped me. The description seemed nothing like the portrayal of early followers of Jesus found in the New Testament.

Early Christians made an incredible difference. Their sacrificial and unrelenting faith turned the world upside down.

My life did not.

> *"No matter how hard I tried, satisfaction eluded me. Outside of my family, friends and career, I longed for a greater sense of purpose in my life."*

I grew up knowing and believing God was important. God was up there somewhere protecting me while I was down here living life the best I knew. I attended church every Sunday until college, when I no longer saw the need. When my older sister was diagnosed with a rare cancer at age 27, I didn't realize the extent of the disease. I was a free spirit living the party life in college. Her funeral broke me and forced me to confront my own mortality.

My brother tried to talk to me about Jesus, but his words made no sense. I returned to college and immersed myself in the party scene to forget my pain.

God got my attention less than a month later. Drunk and exhausted after Greek Week, I decided to rest at my brother's house. Despite my weary state, I left the party around midnight. Midpoint into the two-hour trip, I rolled down the window to stay alert. Gulping fresh air only helped for a few seconds. I slapped my face and sang in my loudest voice, but nothing helped.

The glare of headlights and the blare of a horn jolted me awake. An oncoming car was headed straight for me. I jerked the wheel and barely missed a wreck. I looked over and saw the clock. It read 2:08.

I should have pulled over. Instead, I drifted off to sleep eight or nine more times over the next hour, only to be awakened just in time to miss another possible head-on collision. Somehow, I made it to my brother's house where I crashed on the couch.

The next morning my brother jostled me awake. "Hey, are you okay?"

My head pounded. "Yeah, I'm okay. Why?"

"God woke me up at 2:08 to pray for you." Whoa. I couldn't believe it.

The idea of a personal God was foreign to me. The big guy seemed distant and invisible. But my brother seemed to think Jesus was his best friend. Suddenly my brother couldn't get enough Jesus, church or Bible study.

I couldn't help but wonder. *If Jesus woke up my brother to pray for me, could God be real? Did he have a plan for my life?*

I stayed with my brother and his wife for the summer. He invited me to go to church with them on Sundays, so I agreed.

Each Sunday I heard the pastor share about Jesus in a way that seemed real and personal. Until this honest time of seeking God, I never realized the faith I had was the faith of my parents. I'd never really taken ownership of my faith.

One morning, Jesus got a hold of my heart. When the speaker asked if anyone wanted to surrender his or her life to Jesus, I raised my hand. Peace flooded my emptiness.

God moved from being *important* in my life to becoming the *center* of my life. Wow. What a shift. It's as if I wore a sign around my neck that declared, "Under New Management." With Jesus as the boss, I would now build my life around him and his plans for my life.

I returned to college, and God began a radical change in my life. I quit drinking, stepped down as fraternity president and started leading Bible studies. I didn't know the difference between the Old and New Testament, but I earned a new reputation: Jesus freak.

Fast forward a decade.

Despite my heavy involvement at church, I couldn't shake the growing unrest inside me. Something was still missing.

After much prayer, my wife and I decided to serve in the foreign mission field. I quit my job as a chemical engineer, and we sold everything. We would live anywhere while we prepared to move overseas.

Except the inner city. North Omaha was far too unsafe to raise fourteen children.

But God had other ideas.

If my life in the inner city came with bullet points, the following proved true:

- The crime, violence and brokenness overwhelmed me. Being religious and good was not enough. My neighbors needed more than a *nice* me; they needed the transforming power of Jesus.
- Inviting Jesus into my heart was critical, and yet, it was just the first step. While Jesus gave me personal peace, joy and love, I sensed a purpose beyond myself.

With brokenness surrounding me, I sensed Jesus inviting me into his heart. Empathy and compassion flooded my soul as I felt the pain and heartache Jesus had for people. This was a game changer, and I started living with passion. Like breathing involves inhaling and exhaling, Christianity has two parts: we invite Jesus into our heart, to begin a personal relationship with him. Then, we let Jesus invite us into his heart, giving us purpose. While I'd experienced the personal, I had been missing the purposeful.

My desperation placed me exactly where God wanted me. Being around brokenness had broken me. God is comfortable when I'm uncomfortable. I had to trust him rather than myself. To lean into Christ's supernatural abilities meant admitting my own inabilities. Working hard at living the Christian life wasn't enough. My independence didn't allow God to work.

I'd never thought of Christianity in terms of a *lifestyle;* I thought Christianity was more about having deep convictions and beliefs. I calculated my growth as a Christian by the amount of time spent studying scripture. My head knowledge rarely translated to heart knowledge. The more religious I got, the less relational with unbelievers I became. The more self-reliant I became, the less I depended on God.

I lived with an overwhelming emphasis on having the right set of beliefs in order to truly be a Christian. My engineering background tilted me toward knowledge and understanding. I considered myself a risk-taker when I defended my beliefs and debated right and wrong, but I discovered God's definition looked different. Risk-taking faith was a relational *lifestyle* that attracted people into the arms of Jesus. Sadly, I didn't share my faith on a consistent basis, and very few people became Christians at the church I pastored.

God shook my world and ignited a new love for my neighbors when I moved to the inner city. It's as if I realized I had the cure for cancer, and I wanted to share with everyone. I no longer stood on the sidelines pointing out problems. I saw the faces of hurting people. Brokenness and hopelessness tore my heart.

Revelation 3 warns about lukewarm Christianity. Getting next to brokenness is God's way of heating up our faith until it boils with passion for the lost and hurting in our city. When crime and violence darken the world, the church needs to shine brighter. That meant me.

I can't stay comfortable. God intersects my faith with courage and power when I step out. To live for Christ means getting out of my church seat and into the streets.

I discovered that Christianity has two parts. Inviting Jesus into my heart is a powerful beginning. Allowing Jesus to invite me into his heart is a game changer!

Ron Dotzler is pastor, author, entrepreneur, founder and chairman of ABIDE, and founding pastor of Bridge Church. Learn more about Ron and Bridge Church at www.bridgeomaha.org

Epilogue

Used to Be

There once was a king who changed everything. He didn't stay in his palace aloof from his subjects, but he lived among the people. He taught them his great wisdom. He loved them, prayed with them and touched them. And there was something amazing about his words and his touch.

After people encountered him, they redefined themselves according to what they "used to be." And there were a lot of used to be's who bragged about their encounter with the king:

- Mary—used to be a prostitute
- Bart—used to be blind
- Jairus—used to be a desperate dad
- Matt—used to be an embezzling tax collector
- Zack—used to be an exploiter of the poor
- Sarah—used to be condemned for adultery
- Ben—used to be unable to walk
- Lazarus—used to be dead
- Nick—used to be way too religious
- Samantha—used to be an outcast

They each used to be broken, sick, or hurting. But now their lives have done a 180. Why? King Jesus touched them. Maybe with his hands or maybe with his words.

They used to be a mess. But now, they each claim a new identity: Son of God, Daughter of the Most High. Of inestimable value, Soldier of the thorn-crowned king, Ambassador of the Almighty, New Creation, Clean.

And this kingdom just keeps growing and welcoming new people with their messes, offering hope that anybody who trusts can themselves become a new creation.

The stories in this book are all about people who "used to be" something: an addict, a lost child, hopeless, an atheist. And today, they have a new direction, a purpose and a joy that no circumstance can steal. They've found the God who is within reach.

You can contact or wander into any of the churches listed in this book. You can talk to any of the pastor/authors about finding life. On church websites, Facebook or other social media sites, you can find the people whose lives have been changed. They are all real!

Maybe you will encounter the king... and become a "used to be"!